DARK DUNDEE

INTRODUCTION

If you know us, you may already know that we like our local history punchy, quirky and dark. This book is no exception.

We have thoughtfully collated a selection of stories and tales from Dundee's dark past for your entertainment.

This book is written in an accessible style to appeal to everyone of almost any age and is packed with related facts and figures from Dundee and around the world. It is not intended to be an academic work but we are confident there's bound to be something in this book that you didn't already know.

With that in mind, let's dive in.

CONTENTS

Dark Waters
The Tay Rail Disaster, Tsunami, The Dalhousie, The Tay Whale, William Kidd, Olnik, Toshie

Medical Miseries
Medieval Surgery, Plague, Grave Robbers, Cholera, Lunacy, Forgotten Diseases

Murder & Executions
John Watt, Grissell Jaffray, Patrick Duncan, Thomas Leith, Bridget Kiernan, William Bury, Mark Devlin, Jean Milne

Restless & Unruly
The Tree of Liberty, The Siege of 1651, Mag Gow, Coronation Day Riot, Mary Brooksbank, Stobs Fair

The Supernatural
The Ghost of Blackness, Helen Duncan, The Nine Maidens, Execution of David Balfour, Spring Heels

Morbid Curiosities
Weird & Unusual Deaths, Punishments, Bonnie Susie Cleland, Crimes of the 1500's, Horrors of the Howff

Packed with **GRUESOME,** gory and **GHOULISH** tales and facts. Enter if you **DARE...**

Dark Waters

The mighty River Tay has brought Dundee as much prosperity as it has trouble. For centuries, the busy harbour brought the city most of its wealth, with many of Dundee's seafaring folk travelling the world in search of riches from other lands and seas. Sometimes they brought back the truly unexpected. Sometimes, they didn't come back at all...

120 APPROX **LENGTH IN MILES OF THE RIVER TAY,** THE **LONGEST RIVER IN SCOTLAND**

RIVER SPEY 107MILES; RIVER CLYDE 106MILES; RIVER TWEED 97MILES; RIVER DON 81MILES

 RNLI **BROUGHTY FERRY** is Scotland's BUSIEST Lifeboat Station.

RARE **WILDLIFE**

THE TAY HAS PLAYED HOST AND CONTINUES TO PLAY HOST TO A DIVERSE RANGE OF RARE AS WELL AS DANGEROUS CREATURES, FROM WHALES, BASKING SHARKS, DOLPHINS AND SEALS, TO BEAVERS, STINGING JELLYFISH, SALMON, LAMPREY AND FRESHWATER PEARL MUSSELS, SCOTLAND'S MOST ENDANGERED SPECIES

"ON AVERAGE 50 PEOPLE ACCIDENTALLY DROWN IN **SCOTLAND** EACH YEAR."

SCOTLAND'S DROWNING PREVENTION STRATEGY ROSPA WATER SAFETY SCOTLAND

40+ SHIPS **WRECKED**

There are over 40 known shipwrecks in the Firth of Tay and over 200 in the Tayside coastline!

TREASURES AND VALUABLES TAKEN FROM DUNDEE DURING A SIEGE IN 1651 ARE RUMOURED TO STILL BE BURIED SOMEWHERE IN THE RIVERBED OF THE TAY

175 m³/s VOLUME OUTPUT OF WATER OF THE RIVER TAY, THE LARGEST OUTPUT OF WATER BY ANY RIVER IN THE UK, CALCULATED AT AROUND 175 CUBIC METRES PER SECOND

 RRS DISCOVERY AND **HMS UNICORN** BOTH HAVE THEIR HOMES IN DUNDEE...AND BOTH ARE SAID TO BE **HAUNTED**

THE TAY RAIL DISASTER

In the midst of a terrible storm, a train travelling over the Tay bridge to Dundee plummeted into the murky waters of the River Tay, taking with it every life on board. The events on the evening of 28th December 1879 left an indelibly dark stain on what was first seen as a triumph of modern engineering.

Men, women and children all perished during the disaster, one of the worst in the city's extensive history. Fierce winds tore through the infrastructure of the bridge, collapsing it under the weight of the travelling train, sending both it and its passengers to a watery grave.

SENDING BOTH IT AND ITS **PASSENGERS** TO A **WATERY** GRAVE

Rescue attempts were made but the weather was too troublesome for the rescuers and they were forced to abandon their task until the weather had subsided.

One body washed up on the shore near Newport on 29th December, that of 54 year old Annie Cruickshanks, but the weather was still too severe to risk sending out search vessels.

On 5th January, search parties were sent to help search for the bodies of the estimated 60 or more potential passengers, but this proved to be a longer task than they first thought.

The search continued daily until 27th April 1880, almost 4 months after the disaster. By that point, 13 bodies had still not been recovered from the Tay, perhaps pushed too far out into the North Sea by the mighty current of the river.

BLAME FELL **UPON** THOMAS **BOUCH**

The families of people such as 32 year old John Hamilton, who left behind a wife and 3 children received neither closure nor the bodies of their loved ones.

The final body to be recovered was that of 21 year old William Robertson, a general labourer from Abernethy who was living with a Dundee couple, Mr and Mrs Bain whilst helping to support his father.

The lion's share of the blame fell upon Thomas Bouch, the bridge's main designer and engineer, who tragically died less than a year after the disaster.

THE TAY RAIL DISASTER

46

THE NUMBER OF BODIES RECOVERED FROM THE RIVER AFTER THE DISASTER

The bridge is around 3,264 metres long but can change its length by over a metre due to changes in temperature causing it to expand and contract.

KNIGHTHOOD **STRIPPED** 👑

Thomas Bouch was awarded a knighthood for his services around 10 months prior to the disaster by Queen Victoria. You can bet she snatched that knighthood right back after the grisly horror had unfolded.

All of the carriages were smashed due to the impact of the fall but the engine itself was salvageable and was put back into service with the nickname "**The Diver**". Some recovered artefacts from this dark tragedy are on public display in The McManus: Dundee's Art Gallery & Museum.

THE DAY THE MOST BODIES WERE RECOVERED

07-01-1880

1. John Marshall (24)
2. David Watson (18)
3. William McDonald (41)
4. David Neish (36)
5. James Millar (26)
6. John Sharp (35)
7. Walter Ness (24)

EFFECTS OF THE TIDE

Bodies washed up on the shores of Monifieth, Buddon Ness and Lunan Bay, but the furthest travelled was the body of Joseph Low Anderson, recovered on 23rd April near Caithness coast, close to John O'Groats and over 120 miles away.

ESTIMATED WIND SPEED ON THE NIGHT OF THE DISASTER — **80 MPH**

Decomposition of a body is usually slowed down in water, especially cold water. Any bodies that are found floating are usually face down because the chest cavity has filled with air, but the weight of the body's limbs are acting as anchors and balances.

Adipocere, a hard, soap-like substance also known as grave wax, forms on the body after a few weeks to months of submersion. This process limits bacterial growth and can help further preserve the body. It's a bit late, however, because by this point, you've probably already become part of a seafood buffet for a host of marine scavengers.

"THE BRIDGE ACROSS THE FIRTH OF TAY...WAS REGARDED AS A TRIUMPH **OF ENGINEERING SKILL"**
NEW YORK TIMES, 30TH DECEMBER 1879

⏰ 7:13PM **THE** TIME THE **TRAIN** APPROACHED THE **BRIDGE** ⏰

TSUNAMI

On 1st November 1755, an earthquake hit off the coast of Lisbon. The loss of life was the biggest of any earthquake in recorded history, but not just because of the earthquake itself.

The quake was so large, it produced a tsunami so gigantic and deadly, it didn't only swamp Lisbon and its neighbours but also reached as far as Brazil, Barbados and Greenland. It even graced the shores of Britain on its tour of terror!

When the estimated 20 foot high wave made its way up the Tay and hit the shores of Dundee, the hills all around the area were a blessing, saving the people from being swept away to certain death.

The harbour, its bulwark built from 13th century monastery stones, the piers and all ships berthed there were instantly destroyed by the might of the water.

All storage buildings were entirely overcome as cargo, goods and livestock were swept away by the raging icy torrent.

Buildings remained submerged and it was only once the water had receded that the true damage could be seen.

ALL SHIPS
BERTHED THERE
WERE **INSTANTLY**
DESTROYED

Some of the buildings had required repair prior to the tsunami, but it was clear to everyone that it would take a lot of time and money to rebuild, especially with the threat of another incident like this happening again.

Plans were then made to raise the area higher than the river level using the remaining structures of the old buildings as strong, solid foundations upon which to build.

Thankfully, the harbour continued to prosper after this and, in 1828, a new building, Exchange Coffee House was built on the new elevated site. This building still sits there to this day, currently known as The Shore, a large, ornate building that sits at the very foot of Castle Street, flanked by Exchange Street and Dock Street.

Some of the remains of the old vaulted harbour buildings, an area known as Packhouse Square are hidden from sight underneath this building and are still in considerably good condition for having survived a tsunami!

FLANKED BY
EXCHANGE STREET
AND DOCK STREET

TSUNAMI

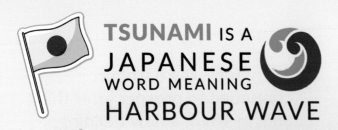

TSUNAMI IS A JAPANESE WORD MEANING HARBOUR WAVE

4 MAIN CAUSES OF TSUNAMI

Tsunami are waves caused by sudden movement of the ocean surface due to:

01 EARTHQUAKES & UNDERSEA QUAKES

02 LANDSLIDES & UNDERSEA LANDSLIDES

03 VOLCANIC ERUPTIONS

04 METEORIC IMPACT

THIS WASN'T OUR FIRST TSUNAMI!

Approximately 8,000 years ago (c. 6,100 BC), a massive underwater landslide in the Norwegian Sea caused a megatsunami which devastated the eastern coastline of Scotland. The wave was believed to be around 21m high. This wave carved out what we now know as the Montrose Basin.

Daniel Defoe is best known as the author of Robinson Crusoe, but he also wrote a 3-volume travel book which was published in the mid 1720's called "Tour Through the Whole Island Of Great Britain". His writings on Dundee can be obtained online from visionofbritain.org.uk.

TIDAL WAVE OR TSUNAMI?
WHAT'S THE DIFFERENCE?

Although both are sea waves, a tsunami and a tidal wave are two different and unrelated phenomena. A tidal wave is a shallow water wave caused by the gravitational interactions between the Sun, the Moon and the Earth. "Tidal wave" was used in earlier times to describe what we now call a tsunami.

"THE INHABITANTS HERE APPEAR LIKE GENTLEMEN, AS WELL AS MEN OF BUSINESS..."

EXTRACT FROM LETTER 13, PART 2: DUNDEE, ABERDEEN & THE HIGHLANDS, DANIEL DEFOE

MEANWHILE, BACK IN LISBON

Looters ran riot. In an effort to send a harsh message to the people, at least 34 looters were hung and their bodies gibbeted on gallows around the town to serve as a warning and a deterrent! Funnily enough, it seemed to do the trick.

THE DALHOUSIE

On the evening of 24th November 1864, the passenger steamer SS Dalhousie found herself in trouble whilst making the coastal journey from Newcastle to Dundee.

After battling for hours against the waves caused by the force-nine gale that raged around them, the steam engines failed in the Tay Estuary, leaving the passengers and crew at the mercy of the elements.

Onshore, shots were heard and distress rockets seen, but with the storm so bad, much like on the night of the Tay rail disaster, search and rescue attempts had to be abandoned. In the dim light of the following morning, everyone's worst fears had been confirmed.

Captain Glenny's body, along with Tom Bisset's, an engineer from Broughty Ferry, were recovered by locals in the Tentsmuir area, having been washed ashore.

The Dalhousie herself was sunk not far from the coast, with just the tips of her masts showing. Wreckage and bodies were strewn all along Tentsmuir beach.

34 people died that night but not all of the dead were washed ashore. Some had to be found by divers with the assistance of helpful locals.

THE **FORCE-NINE** GALE THAT **RAGED AROUND THEM**

TO HELP FERRY THE DEAD AND THE WRECKAGE

2 young girls were found inside the wreck a few days after the tragedy and a woman was found jammed behind a stove in another part of the saloon.

The woman was the wife of a tugboat captain who had offered his ship as a support vessel to help ferry the dead and the wreckage. He had no idea she was on the Dalhousie at the time and was in shock at seeing his dead wife laid before him.

As a diver was searching for more bodies among the wreckage, he had difficulty with what he thought was an overly friendly jellyfish which, in fact, turned out to be the ripped-off scalp of an unfortunate red-headed female passenger.

Despite this added horror, the diver continued with his search until certain there were no more bodies inside the sunken vessel.

Not everyone's bodies were recovered from the water, with the tragedy also creating 18 widows and 52 orphans.

THE DALHOUSIE

The earliest anthropomorphic atmospheric diving suits developed in the 19th century looked like space alien armour and could weigh up to 400kg! The first "diving suit" was produced by John Lethbridge in 1715 and looked like a massive horn with arms!

THE BEAUFORT SCALE

BEAUFORT NUMBER	WIND SPEED (MPH)	WIND DESCRIPTION
0	1	calm
1	1-3	light air
2	4-7	light breeze
3	8-12	gentle breeze
4	13-18	moderate breeze
5	19-24	fresh breeze
6	25-31	strong breeze
7	32-38	near gale
8	39-46	gale
9	47-54	strong gale
10	55-63	whole gale
11	64-72	storm
12	73+	hurricane

£3000 WAS RAISED TO HELP FAMILIES OF THE **VICTIMS** OF THE **DALHOUSIE** DISASTER LEFT WIDOWED OR ORPHANED (WORTH AROUND £380,000 IN 2020)

HURRICANES ARE RATED USING THE SAFFIR-SIMPSON SCALE, WITH RATINGS FROM **CATEGORY 1** (SOME DAMAGE), TO **CATEGORY 5** (CATASTROPHIC DAMAGE)

MORE LIVES TAKEN BY THE DALHOUSIE

Not long after her launch, Dalhousie claimed her first lives. An early morning collision with a much smaller fishing boat called Gleaner left 4 of their 6-man crew dead, 3 of them married with children. No lives were lost from the crew of Dalhousie. An inquiry found that blame lay with Gleaner. Captain Glenny and his crew were absolved of any responsibility in the incident.

THE DALHOUSIE MEASURED 150FT LONG, HAD AN 80 HORSEPOWER ENGINE AND COULD CARRY 30 PASSENGERS, NOT INCLUDING CREW

12TH FEBRUARY **1861** THE DATE DALHOUSIE WAS LAUNCHED

MARY HARTLEY The name of the Broughty Ferry Lifeboat whose crew braved the elements in vain to rescue Dalhousie.

THE GOURLAY **BROTHERS SHIPYARD** DALHOUSIE WAS BUILT AND LAUNCHED HERE. IT WAS SITUATED TO THE EAST OF WHAT IS NOW CITY QUAY (OLD VICTORIA DOCK AND CAMPERDOWN DOCK). IT WAS ONE OF THE BIGGEST SHIPYARDS IN DUNDEE AT THE TIME

CAPTAIN GLENNY IS BURIED IN DUNDEE'S WESTERN CEMETERY

THE TAY WHALE

Contrary to what you may have heard, the Tay Whale didn't just end up washing ashore dead on the banks of the Tay.

He was found dead and floating in the sea near Stonehaven in early January of 1884 after an epic 3 day chase up and down the coast by dozens of whalers.

Many of the whalers were from Dundee, home for the season, and jumped at the chance to capture the beast when it entered the Tay Estuary in late December 1883, drawing crowds of hundreds to the shoreline of Broughty Ferry and kicking off the whale hunt.

Despite having dozens of harpoons fired at it and being chased almost relentlessly for 3 days in a row, somehow the whale gave the whalers the slip. The poor whale died, no doubt from its wounds and exhaustion soon after, on or around 8th January 1884, when it was found and dragged ashore to Stonehaven.

With no harpoons remaining in its side, none of the whalers could legitimately lay claim to owning it, and it was subsequently (and very swiftly) put up for auction.

DOZENS OF HARPOONS FIRED AT IT

Professor Struthers from Aberdeen bid as he wanted to dissect the whale, but an enterprising Dundonian, John Woods, known locally as Greasy Johnny had other ideas. With a limited science budget, Struthers lost the auction.

Greasy Johnny's new sideshow turned out to be a roaring success and after he'd had a couple of weeks of bringing in some cash, Struthers eventually got his hands on the whale. The dissection took place in buildings around the dock area, currently where Exchange Street and Dock Street are in the city.

Never missing an opportunity to make an extra bit of cash, Greasy Johnny sold tickets to the public for the dissection and even hired a band to provide light entertainment during the grisly spectacle.

The impressive beast of the ocean was massive, measuring 40 foot long and was a true sight to behold. However, this particular male Humpback had also been decomposing for over a fortnight.

Not only were Struthers and his team wading about up to their knees in putrid, liquefied whale guts and organs, but they also had to deal with Johnny's audience and an entire band!

To make matters worse, when they tried to extract the whale's heart, it turned to useless jelly in their hands. Thankfully for Struthers, not everything was a total loss and he did manage to find a few semi-intact innards to examine and extract, including its gargantuan stomach.

The skeleton was later gifted to the Victoria and Albert Institute (now The McManus) for reassembly and cleaning and is still currently on display.

LIQUEFIED
WHALE GUTS
AND **ORGANS**

THE TAY WHALE

13 - 14
LENGTH IN METRES OF THE AVERAGE MALE HUMPBACK WHALE

FEMALES CAN GROW ON AVERAGE UP TO 15 - 16 METRES IN LENGTH

10,000 Number of tickets sold to come and see the Tay Whale's body on display in the first day.

The key product of the whale was its blubber. This could be boiled down to produce an oil which was used to light street lamps and lubricate machinery. Blubber was also used in making candles, soap and margarine. In Dundee, it was used to soften the jute for our unrivalled jute empire.

Whale baleen was another popular whale product (the bendy, bone-like substance which a whale uses to filter its food). In the days before plastic, this was a very popular product used in items such as umbrellas, corsets and wide-hooped skirts.

HOW ARE WHALES HUNTED TODAY?

As a whale breaks the surface of the water for air, a harpoon is fired into its head, penetrating up to half a metre deep. As the defenceless whale tries to pull away, a grenade inside the harpoon explodes, blasting shrapnel into its body. If the whale is "lucky" it will die quickly, but often it can take up to an hour or more.

HOW LONG DO WHALES LIVE?

Here's the average lifespan of some of the world's whales:

Killer whale: 50 - 60 years

Blue whale: 80 – 90 years

Sperm whale: 60 – 70 years

Humpback whale: 45 – 50 years

Beluga whale: 35 – 50 years

North Pacific right whale: 70 years

Short-finned pilot whale: 45 years

AND THE BAND PLAYED ON
The band playing throughout the dissection of the Tay Whale weren't just there for entertainment. Medical opinion of the day believed that odours and unhealthy miasma in the air could be eradicated by playing music!

DUNDEE WHALE FISHING COMPANY
The Dundee Whale Fishing Company was the first whaling company to set up in Dundee in the mid 18th century.

"**WHALE** FARTS, LIKE THE ANIMALS THEMSELVES, ARE **EPICALLY** LARGE... RESEARCHERS **CAUGHT** DOWNWIND REPORT IT'S A RATHER **SMELLY** SITUATION"
LIVESCIENCE.COM

1986 THE YEAR COMMERCIAL WHALING WAS BANNED
DESPITE THIS, JAPAN, NORWAY & ICELAND STILL CONTINUE TO DO SO

WILLIAM KIDD

William Kidd, born in Dundee in January of 1654, followed in his father's seafaring footsteps. As an apprentice, he gained many valuable skills, eventually becoming a captain (as the result of a mutiny) and later became part of a small fleet of ships tasked with defending the British colony of Nevis from French attacks. Kidd's new life as a privateer served him very well and he found himself in a world of influential and powerful people.

In New York, he crossed paths with and swiftly married an English woman in her early twenties called Sarah. Widowed twice already, she also happened to be one of the wealthiest women in New York at the time, mainly due to inheritance money from her dead husband.

Unable to stay away from the seas for too long, Kidd soon became tasked with hunting the waters with the intent of attacking anyone who associated with pirates, as well as any French ships because we'd fallen out with them yet again.

Despite his best efforts in the Indian Ocean and the Red Sea, Kidd failed to find any pirates and many of his crew died of cholera.

Finally, in early 1698, Kidd and his crew captured an Armenian ship laden with fine materials, metals and jewels.

A WORLD OF INFLUENTIAL AND POWERFUL PEOPLE

AN **ORDER** WAS GIVEN **TO** **SEIZE** KIDD

Under normal circumstances, the capture of the Armenian ship would have been perfectly acceptable. However, amongst their papers was a document guaranteeing safe passage by order of our reigning monarch King William of Orange.

Once Kidd realised his error, he tried to convince his crew to return the ship, but they refused to comply. News travelled back to England that the Armenian vessel had been pirated and an order was given to seize Kidd and his criminal crew.

Kidd was finally captured in Boston, taken to the Boston Gaol and subjected to what was only described as "extremely harsh conditions".

He stood trial for five counts of piracy and one for the murder of his crew member, William Moore. Two of his own crewmen testified against him in exchange for full pardons from the king.

Kidd was found guilty of all charges, sentenced to death and was publicly hung at Execution Dock in London on 23rd May 1701. His corpse was chained and gibbeted at the mouth of the Thames river then left to rot as an example to others tempted to walk the same path.

WILLIAM KIDD

3,000,000

ESTIMATED NUMBER OF SHIPWRECKS AROUND THE WORLD

> "**IF** THERE'S A MAN **AMONG** YE, YE'LL COME UP AND **FIGHT** LIKE THE MAN YOU ARE TO BE"
> MARY READ

GALLOWS OR GIBBET?

Gallows are a means of execution by hanging using a projected structure from which a person would hang by the neck until they were dead.

A gibbet is any instrument of public execution. The guillotine is an example of a gibbet, as are gallows.

Gibbeting relates to the public displaying of the executed body, and typically happens after death.

There have been cases, however, where people have been gibbeted as a means of execution, being left publicly suspended in cages, chains or rope to die of exposure, thirst or starvation – whichever of the 3 got them first!

GIRLS JUST WANNA HAVE FUN

GRACE O'MALLEY: O'Malley was born into a powerful clan who ruled the coastlines of western Ireland. After taking the helm of the family business in the 1560's, she continued the tradition of plundering English and Spanish shipping vessels and attacking rival chieftains. She was still pirating when she died in 1603 in her early seventies.

ANNE BONNY: Her fierce and courageous temper preceded her and made her stand out as just as good as any of the men in Calico Jack's deadly crew. She later befriended another pirate, Mary Read, whom she led raids with in the Caribbean before being captured by pirate hunters in 1720, alongside Mary, Calico Jack and some others.

MARY READ: Mary fell into piracy after the ship she was working on was attacked by buccaneers. Disguised as a man, she eventually found her way into Calico Jack's crew where she met Anne Bonny and revealed herself to be a woman. When the women were captured during a Caribbean raid in 1720 with their male counterparts, they only escaped execution because they were both pregnant.

3

The number of years William Kidd's body was left hanging in his gibbet.

Also the number of dead husbands Sarah Oort had by the time William's execution had been carried out.

WILLIAM KIDD IS THE ONLY PIRATE KNOWN TO HAVE BURIED TREASURE. TO THIS DAY, NOBODY HAS EVER FOUND IT

MY PIRATE

The nickname given to Sir Francis Drake by none other than Queen Elizabeth I herself. Drake sailed on his most famous voyage from 1577 to 1580, becoming the first English captain to circumnavigate the globe. On that same trip he lost four of his five boats, executed a subordinate for allegedly plotting a mutiny, raided various Spanish ports and captured a Spanish vessel loaded with treasure. A delighted Queen Elizabeth immediately knighted him upon his return.

OLNIK

In November of 1876, Captain Adams of the whaler Arctic brought home from his journeys a man named Olnik, the leader of a small Inuit village somewhere on Baffin Island.

It seemed Olnik was curious to see what life was like outside his village, but Adams had other ideas and was intent on cashing in on Olnik during the whaling off-season at home.

People loved it when the whalers brought back things they had never seen before, from trinkets to polar bears. Adams knew that crowds would gather to see something a little different to what they were used to.

Olnik quickly became a local celebrity, making guest appearances in the Dundee music hall and at sporting and social events across the town. Olnik loved the attention and Adams loved the cash.

Huge crowds gathered to see Olnik perform his latest money-spinner for Adams; a dummy seal-hunt demonstration from a kayak in Victoria Dock. Folk just couldn't get enough of Olnik and the way he handled his harpoon.

THEY HAD
NEVER SEEN
BEFORE

CURSED
OR IN SOME
WAY **EVIL**

As with most things however, the novelty soon wore off and word of some of Olnik's antics were becoming local gossip. The boastful revelation that he had left three wives behind in his home village shocked many.

His conduct was also said to have been very ungentlemanly towards women at a high-society wedding in early 1877; he was ordered out in disgrace long before the dancing had even started!

When the whaling ships were ready to set sail again, Olnik was aboard and returned to his village on 24th August 1877. It was only then that his dark secret was revealed.

One of his three wives was only his wife because Olnik had murdered her husband and had 'appropriated' her! It seemed his people were not too pleased to have him back, believing him to be cursed or in some way evil.

Word spread about Olnik among the whalers and whenever the whaling fleet returned to Baffin Island and Olnik asked to return to Dundee, everyone knew to say no.

OLNIK

Time of year average (mean) temperature

	North Pole (Arctic)	South Pole (Antarctic)
Summer	32°F (0°C)	−18°F (−27.7°C)
Winter	−40°F (−40°C)	−76°F (−60°C)

Negative forty degrees is the temperature where the Fahrenheit and Celsius scales correspond with one another (-40°F = -40°C).

INUIT (THE PEOPLE), INUK (SINGULAR), INUUK (PLURAL)

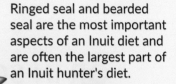

Ringed seal and bearded seal are the most important aspects of an Inuit diet and are often the largest part of an Inuit hunter's diet.

MOST INUIT LIVE IN REGULAR HOUSES, NOT IGLOOS

WHY IS ANTARCTICA COLDER THAN THE ARCTIC?

The Arctic is ocean surrounded by land. The Antarctic is land surrounded by ocean. The ocean under the Arctic ice is cold, but still warmer than the ice! So the ocean warms the air a bit.

Antarctica is dry—and high. Under the ice and snow is land, not ocean. And it's got mountains. The average elevation of Antarctica is about 7,500 feet (2.3 km) and the higher you go, the colder it gets.

1724 The Fahrenheit scale was first proposed by the German physicist Daniel Gabriel. **1724**

1742 The Celsius scale was developed by Swedish astronomer Anders Celsius. **1742**

ANOTHER LOCALLY FAMED INUIT

Almost 50 years after Olnik had departed Dundee for good, another Inuit made local headlines and became briefly famous!

In 1925, Shoodlue was crowned Dundee's Champion Marmalade eater, scoffing a whopping 2lbs of marmalade with bread faster than all the other competitors.

According to Inuit culture in Greenland, a person possesses six or seven souls. The souls take the form of tiny people scattered throughout the body.

A RAMPANT BEAR

IN 1881, A POLAR BEAR CALLED BRUIN RAN AMOK IN DUNDEE HIGH STREET HAVING ESCAPED FROM ITS CAGE DURING TRANSIT TO A MAN NAMED MR WOODS, WHO INTENDED TO SHOWCASE HIM FROM A TENT IN UNUSED GROUND IN COMMERCIAL STREET. THANKFULLY NO-ONE WAS HURT AND BRUIN WAS TEMPTED BACK INTO HIS CAGE AFTER CAUSING QUITE THE SCENE

The lowest natural temperature ever directly recorded at ground level on Earth is −89.2°C (−128.6°F) at the Soviet Vostok Station in Antarctica on 21st July 1983.

68 YEARS
Average life expectancy of an Inuk.

THE INUIT ARE AN INDIGENOUS PEOPLE WHO HAVE LIVED IN THE ARCTIC REGIONS FOR THOUSANDS OF YEARS

TOSHIE

In May of 1884, the crew of the whaler Chieftain leapt into action at the sight of a whale coming up for air in Arctic waters. Jumping into one of four smaller boats deployed to capture their prize, Jamie McIntosh (Toshie) and 4 of his crewmates set off with the other vessels, armed and ready.

With a quick and successful kill under their belts, the 4 boats started to make their return to the Chieftain, with one or two of the boats dragging the dead whale in their wake. Before they'd made it back, a thick fog appeared and the boats soon became blind to each other.

To begin with, it was easy to keep in touch by shouting, but it was clear to Toshie and his shipmates they were drifting away from the group and had lost their sense of direction.

There was no food or water on the boat and the five men, Alick Bain, Willie Christie, Jim Cairns, Willie McGregor and Toshie were alone on the water.

They sailed in circles all through the night trying to find the Chieftain in the impenetrable fog, but to no avail. Exhausted, they had to row their small boat for another 2 full days before finally reaching an ice island.

They did find frozen fresh water which probably saved their lives, but with no food to be found, they had no choice but to set sail again. The next day they saw a ship a couple of miles away, but no matter how much they shouted the much faster ship sailed away, oblivious to their plight.

Their fates were sealed. Willie McGregor died first, having ingested salt water despite knowing the dangers. That same night, Jim Cairns went to sleep and never woke up.

HAD LOST THEIR SENSE OF DIRECTION

THE SAME **WATERY** **FATE** AS HIS DEAD **CREWMATES**

Their bodies were pushed overboard as the clock of mortality ticked for the remaining trio. Willie Christie died next, meeting the same watery fate as his dead crewmates. Toshie wasn't doing too well; his legs had swelled to twice their size from the effects of frostbite.

He had just enough strength to set up the sail as best he could before he fell down, exhausted. Toshie dozed for days, surviving on icicles and the fabric of his bonnet. He was unaware that during the time he had slept, Alick Bain had silently passed away by his side.

Toshie continued to drift in and out of consciousness, barely hanging onto life, when he was miraculously spotted and rescued by the crew of a Danish fishing vessel. The sailors may have managed to save Toshie, but they could not save his legs and they had to be amputated by surgeons onshore in Akureyri, Iceland.

Remarkably, in just a couple of months, he was able to return to Dundee and briefly became a minor celebrity when his story appeared in all the newspapers.

After reading about it, Lord Derby sent him £5 to purchase new wooden legs and someone else gave him a tricycle which he could peddle with his hands. Not only did Toshie use his tricycle for work, but he also cycled to London in 20 days!

TOSHIE

AFTER THE MID 1880's DUNDEE WAS THE ONLY WHALING PORT IN THE UK

Some Dundee whaling ships 'lost' around the world.

Tay I, 1799, **CAPTURED BY PRIVATEERS**

Jane, 1809, **WRECKED**, TAY BANKS

Mary Ann, 1819, **CRUSHED BY ICE**, ARCTIC

Dorothy, 1840, **ABANDONED**, ATLANTIC

Easonian, 1922, **FIRE**, Kekerten CANADA

THE CURSE OF THE TAY
WHALERS I, II & III

After the whaler Tay I was captured by privateers in unknown waters in 1799, her successor, Tay II went on to be crushed by ice in the Davis Strait, the world's broadest strait, between Greenland and Baffin Island in 1819! To make it a hat-trick, Tay III was lost in Melville Bay, off the NW coast of Greenland in 1874. Moral of the story? Don't call your ship "Tay".

£5 in 1884 = approx £635 in 2020

14 Toshie's age when he started whaling. His legs were amputated when he was 28.

A PLAY BASED ON TOSHIE'S LIFE WAS FIRST PERFORMED BY DUNDEE REP THEATRE IN 1994

3 STAGES OF FROSTBITE

Frostbite is damage to skin and bodily tissues caused by exposure to freezing temperatures.

STAGE 1: FROSTNIP
Your body will start to deliver warning signals. You'll experience pins and needles, throbbing or aching in the affected area. Your skin will become cold, numb and white and you may feel a tingling sensation. You should find warmth and shelter immediately.

STAGE 2: SUPERFICIAL FROSTBITE
Further exposure causes top layers of tissues to harden as your skin begins to freeze. Once these tissues thaw, the skin becomes red, blistered and extremely sore. Treatment is essential, but any damage is usually superficial and can be recovered from easily.

STAGE 3: ADVANCED/DEEP FROSTBITE
If exposure continues, your skin becomes white or blue and damage may occur to tendons, muscles, nerves and bones. As your skin thaws, blood-filled blisters will turn into thick black scabs. It's likely that some of your tissue will die and may have to be removed to prevent infection.

THE CHLOROFORM DIDN'T WORK

Toshie stayed alert and awake throughout his amputation despite being given chloroform to put him to sleep. Thankfully he didn't feel a thing - even when a surgeon drove a dagger into the sole of his foot! Toshie watched as they carried his amputated legs away (hopefully not to the kitchen).

Medical Miseries

For centuries the people of Dundee have had to deal with various medical maladies. From leprosy to lunacy, some of the treatments for your ailments could often be as dangerous as they were bizarre. Over the years, the City of Discovery has made many advances in medicine, but we've had our share of misery too.

MEDIEVAL HOSPITALS

In these times, most hospitals in Scotland were church driven and there are records of four medieval hospitals in Dundee. A charter in 1390 granted the Trinitarian Red Friars a building adjacent to their monastery for use as a hospital which sat where Dundee Contemporary Arts is today.

The hospitals of St. John the Baptist and St. Anthony were first mentioned in 1443. The leper house was referred to in 1498 but may have been in existence earlier; leprosy was at its height in the 1100's.

These latter three buildings were all destroyed by an invasion in 1548. The Red Friars building was the only one remaining and was passed into the hands of the Town Council and used as 'a large and splendid hospital for old men' or, in their words, 'decayit auld burgesses'.

Leprosy is a bacterial skin infection causing disfiguring skin sores and lumps, nerve damage in the arms and legs, blindness, muscle paralysis and kidney failure. In 2020, someone was **diagnosed with leprosy every 2 minutes**.

1783
The **CHAINSAW** was **INVENTED** by two Scottish doctors to **HELP WITH CHILDBIRTH**

The polygraph (used as the basis for modern-day lie detectors) was invented by Sir James Mackenzie (1853–1925), a heart specialist who was born near Scone.

DUNDEE DOCTORS

DR DAVID KINLOCH
1560 - 1617
A Dundee doctor, poet and Royal Physician to James VI. In Madrid, he was caught during the Spanish Inquisition but made it home alive.

DR JOHN CRICHTON
1772 - 1860
A skilled surgeon and original Dundee Infirmary doctor. Crichton Street is named after him.

DR GEORGE PIRIE
1863 - 1929
A pioneering researcher in the use of X-rays at D.R.I. Exposure to X-rays caused his hands to be amputated. He also lost one eye and the sight in his other.

DR ALICE MOORHEAD
1868 - 1910
One of the first practising female physicians in Scotland. Established the first all-female practice in Scotland with Dr Emily Thomson at 93 Nethergate.

MODERN HOSPITALS

Dundee Royal Infirmary 1 – Opened 1798 on King Street. Moved in 1855, demolished for dual carriageway.

Dundee Royal Infirmary 2 - Opened 1855, Barrack Road. Closed in 1998. Now housing.

Kings Cross – 1867 temporary smallpox and typhus hospitals built; all demolished for Kings Cross which opened in 1889.

Maryfield Hospital – Opened in 1854 as a poorhouse. Hospital block added in 1891. Closed in 1976.

Royal Victoria Hospital – Purchased by Dundee Town Council to provide a hospital for incurables. Opened in 1897.

Dundee Women's Hospital – Opened in 1915 on Elliot Road. The first private hospital for the treatment of women.

Ninewells – When opened in 1974, it was the first new teaching hospital to be built in the UK since the 1800's.

MEDIEVAL SURGERY

Where Tay Square stands today, in front of the Dundee Rep Theatre, was where the herb garden for the Red Friars Monastery once stood. As well as growing food, they would have grown plants and herbs for medicinal use.

It wasn't just all sage and willow bark; these guys had the good stuff! To tackle pain, ointments were made from honey and opium and then applied to the affected area.

Dangerous plants like belladonna would have been grown too and they may have even made an old anaesthetic called Dwale, used to knock out a patient for surgery.

KNOCK
A PATIENT
UNCONSCIOUS

Dwale was only for extreme procedures such as amputations, because the anaesthetic could be even more dangerous than the surgery.

Black henbane, the opium poppy and hemlock were mixed in a ratio of 3:1:1 and administered to the patient prior to surgery.

One medieval manuscript noted that the potency of the drug was enough to knock a patient unconscious for anywhere between 72 and 96 hours.

Surgery was often performed by monks with little to no experience aside from castrating animals and having access to a few medical books. Educated surgeons were only for the rich.

Pre-amputation, you would be given Dwale and a tourniquet would be applied to limit blood flow. The limb would be raised to further reduce blood flow whilst the surgeon cut through the flesh right down to the bone using a slim, red-hot iron, shaped like a knife.

Damp cloths would be used to cover your flesh and your muscles were pulled back using a lot of effort, so that the surgeon was able to work on your bone using a basic saw. It probably wasn't particularly quick, but once he'd hacked his way through your bone and removed it, that part of the ordeal would be over.

Damp cloths and ointments would be applied to the wound and you would undoubtedly be delirious for days if not weeks afterwards. Death by drug ingestion was just as likely as death by secondary infection from largely unsanitary tools and practises. Risky times.

DELIRIOUS FOR DAYS IF NOT WEEKS

MEDIEVAL SURGERY

Most people in medieval times never saw an actual doctor unless they were very rich. Most were treated by the local wise-woman, monks or the barber who also pulled out teeth, set broken bones and performed other operations. Their cures were a mix of superstition (magic stones and charms were popular), religion (for example driving out evil spirits from people who were mentally ill) and herbal remedies. By the 1500's many 'wise-women' were accused of being witches and put to death.

MEDIEVAL EYE SURGERY

To rid people of cataracts, physicians would use a knife or needle to remove the cataract through the cornea, forcing the lens out of the capsule and to the bottom of the eye. It often led to infection and blindness.

The modern word **"drug"** is derived from the Old English verb **"driggen"** meaning **to dry**, reflecting the preparation of the herbs that would be used in these ancient remedies.

St. Fiacre is known as the "patron of hemorrhoids." He was a seventh century Irish monk who suffered from the disease, sat on a hard rock and was miraculously cured of his illness.

Some medieval doctors would send their patients to sit on the rock for a few hours to cure them of the illness. According to legend, the imprint of St. Fiacre's hemorrhoids remains on the stone today.

It may have been a useless placebo, but it was in no way as painful as the treatment some doled out to their patients. The more scientific monks would insert a red-hot iron tube up the sufferer's rectum!

MEDIEVAL REMEDIES

Buttercups worn in a bag around the neck would cure insanity.

St. John's Wort was most effective for curing fever if found by accident, especially on Midsummer's Eve.

Eating nettles mixed with the white of an egg cured insomnia.

To cure ague swallow a spider wrapped in a raisin.

To cure baldness rub goose droppings over the affected area.

Tie an eel skin around the knee to alleviate cramps.

To cure a toothache, touch a dead man's tooth.

To make freckles disappear, cover them with blood from a bull or hare, or use water distilled from crushed walnuts.

PLAGUE

When the black death swept across Europe in the mid-1300's, the survivors in Scotland called it the Great Pestilence, or The Pest. In the first few outbreaks, not much was known about the disease or how it spread. There are very few records, but estimates claim up to a third of the population died in the 1300's across the country.

Plague is caused by a bacteria, *Yersinia pestis*, usually spread to humans through the bite of fleas carried on rats, but rarely spread from one person to another. For the first few days those infected will have flu-like symptoms, but then signs of plague infection start to set in.

The most common type, bubonic plague, causes painful swollen lymph glands called buboes. Untreated, it can move into the blood causing septicemic plague, or to the lungs causing pneumonic plague – the only form of plague that can be transmitted from person to person.

With a death rate of 60 to 90%, there was no option but to quarantine the infected, who were banished outside the town to recover or die at the 'Sickmen's Yard' outside the East or Cowgate Port.

BANISHED
OUTSIDE THE TOWN

One of the most iconic tales from Dundee's history is that of George Wishart preaching to the plague-stricken in 1544 who were left in the Sickmen's Yard to die. The people of Dundee loved Wishart for this.

Next to nearby St. Roque's Lane, once known by locals as 'semirookie', was St. Roque's chapel and a burial ground for plague victims. St. Roque's was already in ruins by the time Wishart preached near there, and the burial grounds full. Thereafter, plague-stricken were buried in Roodyards.

So many people died in the 1544 plague outbreak that when a call was put out across the country for soldiers, Dundee had no healthy men able to join.

In 1585 when plague hit the town again, officials put orders in place to prevent more outbreaks. Cleaners were hired to deal with the possessions of the dead and to search the goods of merchants, as were quarter-masters who were responsible for searching the homes in their quarter of town every day for signs of infection.

Ships were quarantined for 40 days and all crossings stopped across the Tay. While this helped us avoid an outbreak of plague for a few years, it later struck in 1608 and then again in 1648.

SIGNS OF
INFECTION

PLAGUE

"BETWEEN SIDLAW AND THE SEA, PEST OR PLAGUE SHALL NEVER BE"

An old local saying from around 1600.

Around 40 years after Wishart preached to the plague-stricken, walls were built around the town. The East Gate, or Port, was also rebuilt and called WISHART ARCH. It is still standing to this day.

1900 YEAR OF THE LAST PLAGUE OUTBREAK IN SCOTLAND

IN GLASGOW, RATS CARRYING INFECTED FLEAS ARRIVED VIA INTERNATIONAL SHIPPING ROUTES. 36 PEOPLE WERE INFECTED AND 16 DIED

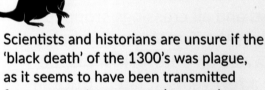

Scientists and historians are unsure if the 'black death' of the 1300's was plague, as it seems to have been transmitted from person to person, whereas plague tends to spread on fleas which travel on rats. Plague can also be spread by the scratch or bite from an infected housecat!

During the outbreak in 1648 estimates are that up to 1,000 people died from a population of around 12,000.

It ruined the local economy. For 4 months from August to November everything in Dundee was closed. Nothing was sold at the markets and those who could, fled the town. Those with no money and nowhere to go, were stuck.

Two young women from the Hilltown turned to an unusual food source to survive... In the years after the plague there were many food shortages. When people saw how healthy these women looked, they accused them of witchcraft. Only then did they reveal they had been feasting on black slugs they had been hoarding in a barrel, opening it to reveal it full of slugs!

People were confined to their homes if they showed any symptoms, but NOT EVERYONE WANTED TO FOLLOW THE QUARANTINE RULES. In 1607 William Strathauchine, a shoemaker, thought the quarter-masters were getting a bit too big for their boots.

The incident is quoted in Maxwell's 'The Old History of Dundee': "[William] abused ane of the quarter-masters appointit to attend upon persons infected, by saying that he had usurpit the office, and be giving him of the lie; and theirefter [sic] provoked him to the combat, and passed to his awn house and returnit seeking him with ane drawn sword."

In the end he was punished along with another fellow shoemaker who joined in, by being made to crave forgiveness at the Town Cross.

THE OVERPAID CLOCK KEEPER

Patrick, the clock keeper, like so many others, fled the plague in 1608. As a result, the clock on the Old Steeple stopped working. When he returned, he demanded extra money to fix it. No one else knew how, and the council were so desperate to get it working again they paid his fee of £40 (equal to £10,000 today!).

GRAVE ROBBERS

In the early 1800's, as medical schools and anatomy departments grew in size and reputation, so did the demand for fresh corpses to dissect.

Only having the bodies of executed criminals to dissect, doctors were willing to pay large amounts of money for fresh bodies, no questions asked, and so the evil trade of grave robbing began.

When bodies started to go missing from their graves in the Logie cemetery on Lochee Road and the Howff cemetery, the town was in uproar and demanded that the council do something about it.

FELL INTO A FRESHLY-DUG GRAVE

They responded by building a guard tower, manned by volunteers. Guards were sometimes armed and would fire their pistols into the darkness in the hope of scaring off a grave robber before giving chase.

Two watchmen were once chasing robbers out of the Howff when one of the men tripped and fell into a freshly-dug grave. When he climbed out, he realised he had tripped over the body of the person who had just been taken out of the grave.

The doctors willing to pay good money for fresh corpses were in Edinburgh, Aberdeen and Glasgow, so Dundee grave robbers would have had to transport the body, a challenging feat in the 1800's. They were paid up to £10 per body (roughly £1,000 in today's terms) so the money was worth it for some.

In 1823, a medical student decided to join the ranks of the grave robbers when he dug up and stole the body of an elderly woman from the Howff cemetery. Stuffing the body in a wooden box, he took her on a coach ride to Edinburgh, to curious looks from fellow passengers.

After lots of questions, the nervous student noticed they were approaching Kinghorn and tried to flee, but he was caught with the grisly contents redhanded.

Other than this incident, no other grave robbers were caught in Dundee. It wasn't until the Anatomy Act of 1832 which gave doctors access to more bodies for dissection that the grisly trade largely stopped.

STUFFING THE BODY IN A WOODEN BOX

GRAVE ROBBERS

AN ACT FOR BETTER PREVENTING
THE HORRID CRIME OF MURDER

The **1752** Murder Act allowed dissection after execution as an extra punishment, but it didn't say it had to be for medical studies.

2015 THE LAST TIME A GRAVE WAS ROBBED IN THE TAYSIDE AREA

3,600 PEOPLE VOLUNTEERED TO WATCH THE HOWFF AT NIGHT

The problem was, they either didn't show or were too drunk, cold or scared. Once they were armed, they got a bit braver. One guard chased a grave robber and as he climbed the walls, the guard shoved his bayonet in the robber's bum but didn't manage to catch him.

The most unscrupulous would **MURDER** to obtain a fresh body. Burke and Hare were not the first; that honour goes to Helen Torrence and Jean Waldie who were executed after murdering a 9 year old boy in 1751 in Edinburgh and selling him to the surgeons.

ZOMBIE CAGES AND EXPLODING COFFINS

Some went to great lengths to see that bodies remained securely in their graves. Mortsafes were metal cages (or half cages) put around a grave. Mortsafes could be permanent (which was expensive) or hired as an iron grid called a press. It was buried on top of the coffin and returned once the body had sufficiently decayed. One Dundee father took it to extremes when burying his daughter.

The coffin had wires attached, which he said were rigged to explosives so that if anyone tried to steal her body, they would be blown to bits!

TOP TIPS FOR GRAVE ROBBERS

PACK LIGHT
You only need a lamp, a sturdy shovel and some rope - that body is likely to be heavy!

KNOW YOUR NUMBERS
Make sure the death is recent, but also check the age of your victim; you'll be paid less for a child.

AIM HIGH
Digging up the whole grave takes too much time. Dig a small hole near the headstone. Use your shovel to smash through the coffin, and then your rope to heave the body out of the ground.

Geordie Mill was a gravedigger whose neighbour Donald McNab suspected he had been grave robbing. There was no evidence, but he did get a song written about him.

It was more of a crime to be caught with stolen cloth than it was to steal a corpse! Stealing cloth was an offence punishable by hanging, so it made sense to strip a body down before moving it. Nobody had ever been executed solely for stealing a dead body, but many had hung for stealing the clothes from a dead person!

DITCH THE CLOTHES!

CHOLERA

Several outbreaks of cholera hit Dundee in the 1800's, mainly due to overcrowding, living conditions and poor sanitation. Cholera is caused by bacteria that spreads in water contaminated with faeces from an infected person.

If it gets into the drinking supply it spreads quickly through communities. It causes diarrhoea leading to fatal dehydration. People lived in very close quarters and didn't know about hygiene. They believed bad smells caused diseases.

Overcrowding in the poorest areas meant up to 12 people could share a bed. With people living in such close quarters, once one person was infected, the disease would rapidly spread to the rest of the family. Without access to modern conveniences like washing machines, keeping anything clean was and hygienic was next to impossible.

Toilets in the early 1800's were outdoors in an outhouse and shared with several other households. They were rarely cleaned, so most people still used a 'chamber pot', but this was often just a bucket in the corner.

CAUSES FATAL DEHYDRATION AND DIARRHOEA

People were supposed to bring their waste downstairs to a communal pile. Most people still used the old 'guarde loo' method and emptied their buckets out of their windows onto the streets below.

People constantly complained about the awful smell of animal innards and flesh from butchers and fishmongers in addition to the huge volumes of excreted animal waste piling up in the streets. To get rid of the smell, rotting waste was often dumped in nearby streams, contaminating our water supply. People still mainly used communal wells which became filthy and infected.

ANIMAL WASTE PILING UP IN THE STREETS

The worst outbreak of cholera was during the 1832 pandemic, but at that time they didn't have a clue how to cure it!

A tenement building at the bottom of Union Street was used as a cholera hospital to treat the infected. The overuse of some of their treatments could dehydrate you further, increasing your risk of death.

Over a period of 30 weeks 800 people were infected in Dundee, 512 of whom died.

CHOLERA

TIPPING THE BUCKET

In Dundee we had a polite way of emptying out a chamber pot into the streets. In some other towns, a forceful throw was used to ensure as much waste arced away from you as possible. Our streets were narrow; doing it that way meant if your neighbour across the road had her window open, it could end up inside her house! The polite method was to tip, not chuck, ensuring the waste went straight down onto the street. So thoughtful!

THE CHOLERA PIT

During the biggest Dundee outbreak in 1832, the population was about 40,000. Over 30 weeks, the 512 additional deaths just from cholera was more than our gravediggers could handle. A mass grave was dug known as the Cholera Pit, where most of these 512 people were buried underneath what is now a path on the south side of the Howff cemetery.

80% OF PEOPLE DO NOT DEVELOP CHOLERA SYMPTOMS
THE INFECTION RESOLVES ON ITS OWN
1/5 OF THE REMAINING 20% HAVE SEVERE DIARRHOEA, VOMITING, LEG CRAMPS, AND DEHYDRATION, CAUSING SEPTIC SHOCK AND DEATH

THERE HAVE BEEN 7 CHOLERA PANDEMICS IN THE LAST 200 YEARS

19TH Nov:
WORLD TOILET DAY
An event hosted by the **World Toilet Organization** to raise awareness for the 2.5 billion people around the world who live without access to a proper toilet.

AN EPIDEMIC is a disease that affects a large number of people in a community, population, or region. A PANDEMIC is an epidemic that has spread over multiple countries or continents.

There was some method to piling up poo in the street. There were two piles, one for animal waste and one for humans. Each week or so it would be cleared away.

The local kids loved playing in the piles of poo, but just the human ones because in there they might find a bit of rag or bone or a wee treat to bring home to mum!

LUNACY

The Dundee Lunatic Asylum opened in 1812 on Albert Street, which was outside the town boundaries at the time. Only three patients were admitted when it opened but the numbers swelled over the years until the building became unfit for purpose. A new asylum was built at Liff in 1882 and the old building was demolished.

Life was not easy; people expressed the same feelings of doubt, grief and mental anxiety that we still see today in modern society. Unfortunately for those sent to the asylum in these times, proper diagnosis and treatments were just not available.

FEELINGS OF DOUBT, GRIEF AND MENTAL ANXIETY

Many patients were suffering from physical diseases affecting the mind and brain which we can easily treat with drugs today. Because the underlying conditions weren't treated, asylum stays lasted months or years with no end in sight for some patients.

What people did get from the asylum was palliative care. Although there are stories of mistreatment or misdiagnosis, many were relieved to be admitted as they had no other option or were unable to take care of themselves.

Even those suffering from extreme grief were able to be admitted to the asylum for short periods, receiving care and attention until their emotional pain became more manageable.

In the Dundee Lunatic Asylum records there are a number of curious cases classed as "cured" after very short periods of time, such as a 49 year old man who was admitted in the 1840's expressing "severe homicidal mania". He spoke of intense desires to cut the throats of his wife and children, but he was deemed cured and released back to them within 3 months.

Another case involved a female patient who was diagnosed with the unusual condition "demonomania".

She talked of seeing the devil and his "imps", the "devil coming to carry her away" and of being "sold to the devil". A large abscess appeared on her lips around this time. After 7 weeks the abscess burst and miraculously all her symptoms disappeared! She was certified as cured and released back to her family soon after.

CUT THE THROATS OF HIS WIFE AND CHILDREN

LUNACY

In Britain at the beginning of the 1800's there were a few thousand **"lunatics"** housed in a variety of institutions. By the beginning of the 1950's there were over 150,000.

I've seen the Asylum they lately have made,
And approve of the plan, but indeed I'm afraid
If they send all the people of reason bereft
To this Bedlam, but few in the town will be left.
For their passions and drink are so terribly strong
That but few here retain all their faculties long.
And with shame I must own, that the females, I think
Are in general somewhat addicted to drink.
In reference to the Dundee Lunatic Asylum, written by Thomas Hood.

MEDIEVAL
MENTAL HEALTH

We know very little about the early history of mental health treatment in Scotland. There are mentions prior to the 1700's that treatments were of a 'crude, rough and ready nature' and there are also records of 'the whipping of the mad'. There are some references to folk remedies but, before the asylums, those with serious mental health issues were treated in the same way as criminals and left to rot in prisons.

MONTROSE ROYAL LUNATIC ASYLUM
THE FIRST IN SCOTLAND
OPENED IN 1782

Previously, those with mental disorders had been gruesomely exhibited in institutions, imprisoned in cells or chained to walls in workhouses. Some hospitals made money agitating the patients for onlookers.

THE EVER-ELUSIVE CURE

In some cases a patient was never deemed cured and would be transferred to another institution such as the asylum at Cupar or Montrose. A 35 year old male was admitted displaying extreme delusions coupled with intense violence. He had been in and out of prisons and asylums since the age of 27 and truly believed that "the Divine King" had commissioned him to commit acts of violence. He was noted to "besmear his face with excrement" and also tried to have "sexual intercourse with a male nurse". Wandering about his room naked, he would complain that his clothes smelled of blood. He was transferred to the asylum at Cupar as uncured.

FORGOTTEN DISEASES

Just one hundred years ago the people of Dundee were terrified of diseases that are largely forgotten today. Every month, The Courier would report on the latest zymotic disease figures, both cases and deaths. Zymotic diseases is an old term for infectious diseases.

In most years back then over a third of deaths were due to infectious diseases. Nowadays they account for around 5% or less of all deaths.

VACCINATION WAS COMPULSORY BY 1864 IN SCOTLAND

Smallpox is a contagious and disfiguring disease with a 30% death rate. It was feared throughout history on the same scale as plague and leprosy. There is no cure, although this was the first disease for which a vaccine was available and vaccination for smallpox was compulsory by 1864 in Scotland.

Unfortunately, medical care was inconsistent. Not everyone received the vaccine and this meant there were still outbreaks. In 1871 there were 375 deaths in Dundee from smallpox alone, which was 11.5% of all deaths that year.

Diphtheria seems to be a truly forgotten disease with many never having heard of it. It was the 3rd biggest killer of children in the 1930's and was known as the 'children's plague'. Spread through the air or from contact, plaques build up in the throat constricting the airways and killing up to 30% of those who contract it.

Fevers (usually scarlet and typhus) were also a big problem and Dundee opened a fever hospital (Kings Cross) to deal with them. There, as well as treating patients, they would also clean people and bake their clothes in a specialised oven to sterilise them and get rid of any lingering lice, nits or other bugs.

One of the most recent and often forgotten outbreaks are the polio cases of the 1940's – 1960's. In a small number of cases, polio can cause paralysis and can kill, yet there's still no cure. Polio struck Dundee in 1947 with 43 cases and 4 deaths; again in 1950 (157 cases and 9 deaths) and again in 1962, mainly in the Fintry area, with 40 cases and 1 death.

In that final outbreak, a vaccine became available and over a period of days, 75,000 people queued at the Nelson Street and Forester Street clinics. At its peak, 3,392 people were vaccinated in just 2 hours!

KNOWN AS THE
CHILDREN'S
PLAGUE

FORGOTTEN DISEASES

Not all outbreaks ended in numerous deaths. The Courier, reporting on the outbreak of mumps in 1925, noted that over 50% of children were off sick with mumps in some schools and that "The epidemic will probably have an adverse affect on the efforts of the children's choirs at Dundee Music Festival"!

8ᵀᴴ MAY 1980

THE 33rd WORLD HEALTH ASSEMBLY
OFFICIALLY DECLARED THE WORLD
FREE OF SMALLPOX

Eradication of smallpox is considered the biggest achievement in international public health.

CONSCIENTIOUS OBJECTION

The term "conscientious objection" was coined in the 1890's in reference to objections to mandatory vaccinations, but during the 20th century the term became generally known as "the objection, for reasons of conscience, to participating in war and military service".

In 1883, hooping (whooping) cough was the BIGGEST CHILD KILLER. It caused 275 deaths in Dundee across the year, almost all of whom were under 5.

THE FIRST VACCINES

It was known for centuries that survivors of smallpox were protected from subsequent infection. Trying to induce a minor form of the disease was called variolation. It involved inhalation of the dried crusts of smallpox scabs or the introduction of pus from a lesion into a scratch on the skin.

Edward Jenner published a study in 1798 showing that inoculation with cowpox protected against subsequent smallpox infections. His ideas were initially met with violent opposition but in time his technique became known as "vaccination" from the Latin name for cow "vacca". The dangerous practice of variolation was forbidden by Act of Parliament in 1840.

VACCINE

THE FIRST ANTI-VAXXERS

The Scottish Anti-Vaccination League was formed in 1896 to coordinate lobbying activities and provide legal advice and support to those prosecuted for non-vaccination.

In the late 1890's, the hub of anti-vaccination in Dundee was a vegetarian café in the city centre. Many vegetarians were anti-vaccination because calf lymph was used in the process of making the vaccines.

MYCOBACTERIUM LEPRAE
The bacteria which causes leprosy.

YERSINIA PESTIS
The bacteria which causes plague.

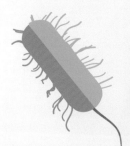

VIBRIO CHOLERAE
The bacteria which causes cholera.

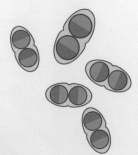

VARIOLA VIRUS
Two types, variola major and minor cause smallpox.

CORYNEBACTERIUM DIPHTHERIAE
The bacteria which causes diphtheria.

POLIOVIRUS
The virus which causes polio.

STREPTOCOCCUS PYOGENES
The bacteria which causes scarlet fever.

MEASLES MORBILLIVIRUS
The virus which causes measles.

Murder & Executions

If you were unfortunate enough to live a few hundred years ago, you could find yourself executed for minor crimes and things we wouldn't think of as crimes today. As times changed, only murderers were executed, but many of them still managed to escape the hangman's noose.

106
NUMBER OF COUNTRIES IN THE WORLD WHERE THE DEATH SENTENCE IS NOW ILLEGAL
Amnesty International 2019 figures.

Described by the Manchester Guardian in 1883 as "...one of the foulest crimes on record", David Urquhart was spared execution for the brutal murder of his 2 year old daughter in Dundee in February of 1883 and instead was sentenced to 21 years servitude.
DAVID URQUHART

"There are still to be found persons who **profess** that when **one murder** has taken place, another **should** follow."
Dundee Courier, 1889

The number of steps leading you to the gallows.
13

1889
Dundee's last hanging was of William Bury on 24th April 1889 for the murder of his wife Ellen.

1963
Scotland's last hanging was of Henry Burnett on 15th August 1963 for the murder of merchant seaman Thomas Guyer.

HUNG, DRAWN AND QUARTERED
The convicted traitor was fastened to a hurdle or wooden panel and drawn by horse to the place of execution.

He was then hanged almost to the point of death, had his genitals cut off and was disembowelled alive before being beheaded and his body then chopped up into four pieces. William Wallace met this exact fate on 23rd August 1305.

Women were spared this fate and were subject to the more 'humane' execution of being burned alive at the stake. Fun times!

HANGING WAS FINALLY ABOLISHED IN THE UK IN 1969 (1973 N.IRELAND)

POLICE ACT GIVEN ROYAL ASSENT FOR DUNDEE. PROFESSIONAL POLICE NOW ON THE STREETS AND A POLICE COURT ESTABLISHED TO DEAL WITH PETTY CRIME AND FINES. LARGER CHARGES WERE LEFT TO THE CIRCUIT COURT
1824

MURDERING SCOTSMEN?
From Monday to Saturday, within the medieval walls of the city of York, it is legal to murder a Scotsman – but only if he is carrying a bow and arrow. Don't bother planning to take advantage of this loophole in the law by taking your disliked relatives to York for some archery; the law was abolished in 2013.

JOHN WATT

In 1801, John Watt was shown the full wrath of the law as he was sentenced to death by public hanging. This led to public outcry, but also stirred up feelings of morbid curiosity.

A change in the law in 1801 meant that criminals were to be executed in the places they committed their crimes instead of their place of sentencing. Dundee hadn't witnessed a public execution in over a century, making this quite the event.

It was said that over 10,000 people watched the execution, which took place outside the Town House, once situated at the front of Dundee's current City Square.

A DWINDLING AND HORRIFIED CROWD

Anyone hoping for a quick execution was out of luck. The rope used to hang John was only a few feet long. After around half an hour, John eventually died in front of a dwindling and horrified crowd.

His body was left hanging outside the Town House for another half an hour acting as a very public deterrent whilst Provost Alexander Riddoch and other magistrates celebrated in a nearby inn on the public purse.

JOHN WATT'S CRIME?
HOUSEBREAKING & THEFT

JOHN WAS A **TAILOR** AND, HAVING NO INCOME AND NO MEANS TO MAKE AN **INCOME**, HE BROKE INTO A **HOME** IN THE NETHERGATE AREA OF THE TOWN AND STOLE SOME **CLOTH**

ALEXANDER RIDDOCH

Provost of Dundee for many years, died in his Nethergate home on 9th December 1822, aged 78 and is buried in the Howff cemetery.

1872 WILLIAM MARWOOD

In 1872, William Marwood introduced a way of calculating the drop length based on height and weight.

BETTER LATE THAN NEVER!

26,000

POPULATION OF DUNDEE IN 1801 WHEN **JOHN** WATT WAS EXECUTED

BASED ON THESE FIGURES, THAT WOULD MEAN THAT THE EQUIVALENT OF AROUND 40% OF THE POPULATION OF DUNDEE WENT TO SEE THE HANGING

SHORT DROP OR LONG DROP?

The short drop method of hanging used little rope for the drop and was a slow and painful death, taking anywhere from a few minutes to upwards of 45 minutes to die. The long drop method started to be used from the 1850's onwards as a more humane execution method; the idea of snapping the neck offering a quicker, less painful death. The technique was further refined by Marwood's findings.

CRIMES THAT COULD HAVE YOU EXECUTED IN THE EARLY 1800's INCLUDED GRAVE ROBBERY, HOUSEBREAKING, STEALING HORSES AND PICKPOCKETING

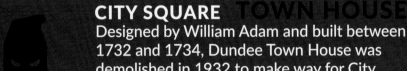

CITY SQUARE TOWN HOUSE

Designed by William Adam and built between 1732 and 1734, Dundee Town House was demolished in 1932 to make way for City Square. The council and guildry chambers were on the first floor with the jail above. This is why executions took place here from the east window of the guildry hall, until the new jail was built on Bell Street in 1837.

GRISSELL JAFFRAY

In November of 1669, three leading figures of the Dundee Presbytery ordered the arrest of a woman, Grissell Jaffray, on charges of witchcraft.

Taken from her city centre home and dragged to the Tolbooth for imprisonment, ministers William Rait, Harry Scrimgeour and John Guthrie approved the employment of a witch pricker as a way of extracting a confession from the aged woman.

After enduring a number of visitations by the witch pricker, Grissell, believed to be in her late sixties to early seventies, finally 'confessed' to her alleged crimes after nine days of incarceration.

In times such as these, a confession of this sort meant only one thing; certain death.

The few remaining records documenting this event state that Grissell was sentenced to be wirried, drowned and then put to the stake to be burned to ash by the 'good people of Dundee' on 21st November 1669.

DROWNED
AND THEN PUT TO
THE STAKE

Many people believe or have been told that Grissell met her fiery fate in the Seagate, where mosaics representing fire and water sit at the top of Peter Street.

There's also a legend that states she was burned at the Mercat (or market) Cross in the Seagate, but in Grissell's time, the Mercat Cross sat across from where City Square now stands, close to the site of the Tolbooth in which she was jailed.

There was a great patch of land just beyond where the West Port now lies. The ground rises up and dips sharply back down, forming a formidable-sized natural basin.

The area was called the Playfields but during the times of the witch hunts, it was known as Witches Knowe or Witchknowe.

It is there where it is most likely Grissell was taken to be burned, as it is believed this is where the town of Dundee burned heretics, sorcerers and witches from as far back as the late 14 to early 1500's.

Grissell was the last woman to be burned at the stake as a witch in Dundee and whilst her records are very sparse, there are at least some to go by.

IT WAS **KNOWN** AS WITCHES KNOWE OR WITCHKNOWE

GRISSELL JAFFRAY

A COMMON MYTH

In the Howff there is a small, columnar piece of stone that was once used by members of the 9 Trades of Dundee. It is mistakenly believed to mark the final resting place of Grissell Jaffray. As she was burned to ash in a public place in November, we can imagine the weather wasn't ideal for sweeping up ashes, never mind then taking them to a religious burial ground.

1486

MALLEUS MALEFICARUM (HAMMER OF WITCHES) PUBLISHED, WRITTEN BY GERMAN CLERGYMAN HEINRICH KRAMER

MARGARET COULL WAS BELIEVED TO HAVE BEEN OUTED AS A WITCH BY GRISSELL JAFFRAY IN HER 'CONFESSION'. DESPITE THE CHURCH'S EFFORTS TO GAIN PERMISSION FOR HER EXECUTION WITHIN 6 MONTHS OF JAFFRAY'S, SHE WAS SPARED DEATH AND WAS INSTEAD GIVEN A BANISHMENT FROM THE PRESBYTERY'S BOUNDS.

"**SEDUCED** BY THE **DEVIL** IN DREAMS AND **VISIONS**"

CANON EPISCOPI (ON THE MATTER OF WITCHES), 900 AD

Between 1484 and 1750, some 200,000 witches were tortured, burned or hanged in western Europe. Most were women – many of them old, vulnerable and poor. By 1563, witchcraft had been made a capital offence in England, Scotland, Wales and Ireland.

GRISSELL JAFFRAY WAS BORN IN ABERDEEN TO A QUAKER FAMILY AND MARRIED JAMES BOUTCHARD, A MERCHANT IN DUNDEE

HYPATIA OF ALEXANDRIA

The oldest witch trial on record is that of Hypatia, born around 355 AD in Alexandria (a port city in Egypt founded around 331 BC). A leading mathematician and astronomer due to the teachings of her father Theon, Hypatia found herself accused of witchcraft in her later years.

In 415 AD, aged around 60, Hypatia was attacked by a mob whilst riding a chariot. Using razor-sharp shells, the mob flayed Hypatia alive before burning her remains and destroying her works in an attempt to erase her from history entirely. Thankfully it failed, and Hypatia's memory lives on.

1590 THE START OF THE NORTH BERWICK WITCH TRIALS WHICH LASTED 2 YEARS AND IMPLICATED 70 PEOPLE

Forms of torture used to extract confessions included leg crushers, thumbscrews and the Pear of Anguish (you should look that one up).

Burning at the stake was a traditional form of execution for women found guilty of witchcraft. Most accusations of witchcraft, however, did not originate in the church but resulted from personal rivalries and disputes.

BLOOD STILL ON HIS HANDS

On the evening of 11th April 1829, in their home in the Blackness area of Dundee, Patrick Duncan drove an axe numerous times into his wife's head, murdering her. After the deed, he retired to bed.

The body was discovered the following day by a young woman, Isabella Buick, who visited the property to run errands for Mrs Duncan. When Patrick denied her entry to the house, she barged in, made the shocking discovery and then fled the house in terror.

Police officers entered the house, saw the bloodbath before them and arrested a calm but clearly confused Patrick Duncan, his wife's blood still on his hands.

It was clear that more than an axe had been used on Mrs Duncan's body, with medical examiners noting that it looked as though Patrick had tried to cut his wife's head off with some kind of knife.

The jagged cuts in Mrs Duncan's throat and neck were so deep they exposed bone, flesh and sinew. Her head hung onto its precarious position by sheer virtue of her unsevered spinal column.

A quick search of the property revealed a blood and gore covered penknife, but any attempts to get Patrick to make any sense were not proving as fruitful.

Whilst he admitted to the murder of his wife, he claimed that she held him in their home against his will, which prevented him from doing his job as the Lord Mayor of Dundee.

Character witnesses testified that the Duncans were heavy drinkers, with Mrs Duncan also said to be at her wits end over her husband's behaviour, which, in the past had included suicide attempts and public endangerment of life.

Patrick's daughter from his first marriage testified to her father's ongoing mental health issues, undoubtedly saving Patrick from the hangman's noose which he was otherwise most certainly destined for.

Instead of the death penalty, he lived out the remainder of his years in the lunatic asylum of Dundee, still convinced his wife was out to get him and equally as convinced he was the Lord Mayor.

SHE **HELD** HIM IN THEIR HOME AGAINST HIS **WILL**

PATRICK DUNCAN

Overcrowding and poor sanitation were serious issues in asylums, which led to movements to improve care quality and awareness. At the time, the medical community were not as enlightened as they are today and often treated mental illnesses with brutal physical methods such as ice water baths, bloodletting, electroconvulsive therapy and ice-pick lobotomies.

SOME PEOPLE WHO AVOIDED THE DEATH PENALTY IN DUNDEE

CATHERINE SYMON
CHILD MURDER
Sentenced: 30th April 1841
Life - Town House Prison.

BRIDGET KIERNAN
CHILD MURDER
Sentenced: 13th April 1860
Life - Town House Prison.

ALEXANDER HUTCHESON
SPOUSAL MURDER
Sentenced: 26th April 1861
Life - Dundee Prison, Bell St.

THOMAS SCOBIE
MURDER
Sentenced: 8th April 1873
14 years - Dundee Prison, Bell St.

One of the **EARLIEST** forms of treatment for mental illness, **trephination** (also called **trepanation**) involved opening a hole in the SKULL using an auger, bore, or even a **saw**. It is estimated THAT this treatment began **7,000** YEARS ago.

"Further, public scandal, and all unpleasant discussion respecting the private affairs or strange conduct - often originating from disease - of individuals, especially if moving in the upper classes of society, will be effectually obviated." Extract from "Notes of a Visit to the Public Lunatic Asylums of Scotland", John Webster.

"UP UNTIL THE SECOND
HALF OF THE 19TH CENTURY PATIENTS WERE **MANACLED** TO OUTHOUSES **CHAINED** TO THE WALL AND **FORCED** TO LIE IN THEIR OWN EXCREMENT.
Lunatics, Imbeciles and Idiots: A History of Insanity in Nineteenth-Century Britain & Ireland.

The **Dundee** Lunatic ASYLUM was officially opened in April 1820 and was designed by William Clark. In 1819, the Dundee Lunatic Asylum formed part of the Dundee Royal Infirmary and Asylum and in 1820 it was formally established as a separate entity - the Dundee Lunatic Asylum - in premises in the Stobswell area of the town (Dundee didn't become a city until 1892). In 1875 it received a Royal Charter from Queen Victoria and became the Dundee Royal Lunatic Asylum.

THOMAS LEITH

PUMP HER STOMACH OF ITS CONTENTS

On 21st April 1847, Ann Leith and her children became very ill after eating breakfast porridge in their home in the West Port area of Dundee.

Reverend James Johnston found the family in a state of severe distress and immediately ran to the shop downstairs where Ann's estranged husband Thomas worked and lived.

He sent Thomas to find a doctor but when Thomas didn't reappear, set off to find one himself. By the time Dr Crichton arrived on the scene, the children appeared to be somewhat better but Ann was dangerously close to death.

Doubtful that porridge could have caused her to become so violently ill, he forced a rubber tube down Ann's throat and began work to pump her stomach of its contents with little success as her shocked children and the Reverend looked on.

Dr Crichton tried to pump her stomach a second time but three hours after eating her breakfast, Ann Leith was dead on her living room floor. Everyone was suspicious of Thomas, who, despite being financially sound, barely gave her enough money to feed herself and their six children.

Dr Crichton had diagnosed arsenic poisoning and Reverend Johnston went on record to state that Thomas Leith had confessed to him that he wanted to divorce his wife. Leith protested his innocence but was arrested. In the absence of any real evidence, he was swiftly tried for her murder.

Shockingly, it only took the jury 90 minutes to decide that Thomas was guilty. Clemency from the death penalty was sought but not granted.

Thomas Leith was duly executed for the murder of his wife; the public convinced that not only was he guilty of her murder but that he had also attempted to murder his children.

He was publicly executed in front of a crowd including his children on 5th October 1847.

HE WANTED TO DIVORCE HIS **WIFE**

THOMAS LEITH

THE 5 DEADLIEST POISONS & WHAT THEY DO TO YOU

BOTULINUM
Ingest this and you will die in extreme pain as your nervous system fails.

RICIN
Chewing just a few castor beans can cause respiratory and organ failure as well as death within hours.

ANTHRAX
Inhaling anthrax will give you flu-like symptoms that do not go away. This is your respiratory system collapsing.

SARIN
Sarin is hundreds of times more toxic than cyanide. Exposure to the gas will cause coma and death.

TETRODOTOXIN
Otherwise known as pufferfish venom. Causes paralysis and death. There's enough toxin in one fish to kill 30 adult humans.

8am TIME OF THOMAS LEITH'S EXECUTION ON 5TH OCTOBER 1847

BY 11AM, THE SCAFFOLDING WAS DOWN AND IT WAS BACK TO BUSINESS AS USUAL AS THOUGH NOTHING HAD EVER HAPPENED

12 The number of children Ann and Thomas Leith had, although sadly only 6 were surviving at the time of their mother's death (murder?)

ISABELLA KENNEY Leith's mistress, who turned up to give evidence at his trial and revealed that she had bore him a child called David on 15th March 1847 in Forfar.

WHAT DO NAPOLEON BONAPARTE AND ANN LEITH HAVE IN COMMON?
THEY ARE BOTH SUSPECTED TO HAVE DIED FROM ARSENIC POISONING

12,000 The NUMBER of people ESTIMATED to have ATTENDED LEITH'S execution, with REPORTS of up to as many as 15,000.

"HIS STRUGGLES WERE OF BRIEF DURATION; A LITTLE MOTION OF THE HANDS, A SLIGHT TWITCHING OF THE SHOULDERS, AND ALL WAS OVER. AT ABOUT NINE O'CLOCK THE BODY WAS CUT DOWN."

EXTRACT OF DUNDEE COURIER REPORT ON THOMAS LEITH'S EXECUTION, 1847

THOMAS LEITH WAS EXECUTED IN THE GROUNDS OF DUNDEE PRISON, BELL STREET

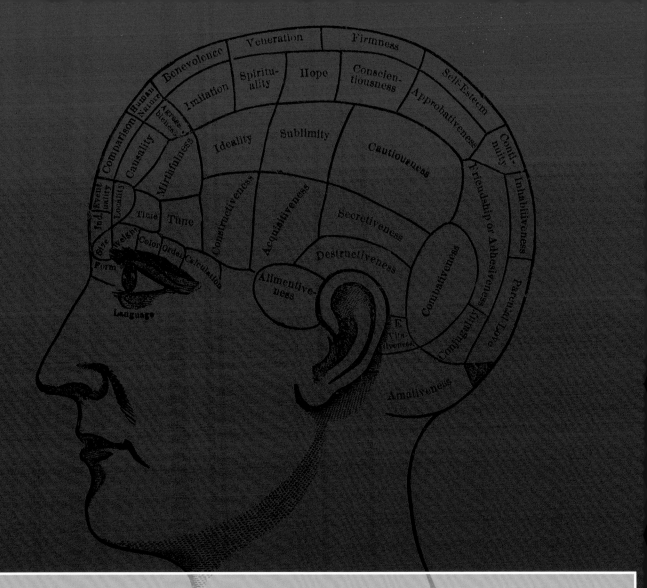

PHRENOLOGY - the study of the shape and size of the cranium to predict mental traits.

A cast of Thomas's head was sent to the secretary of the Dublin Phrenology Society, John P Wright, who had a few things to say about Thomas based on his observations:

"In short, my opinion decidedly is – that he was an exceedingly vain, coarse-minded, cunning, dishonest character. Of course I don't say he absolutely poisoned his wife, nor do I say he told a lie when about to be swept into eternity; but my conviction is, that from his unquestionably deficient conscientiousness – his excessive love of approbation – his great secretiveness, and active combativeness – he both could and would persist in a falsehood to the very last moment of his life."

BRIDGET KIERNAN

In November of 1859, Bridget Kiernan was trying to get her 7 month old daughter Mary to breastfeed, but was having no success.

Thinking the child was in some way ill, she gave some castor oil to her and attempted to breastfeed once again. Bridget's landlady, upon returning home and hearing a commotion, checked on Bridget and Mary only to see the baby's face was blue and her eyes were rolling in her head.

She fled the property in shock to find a doctor whilst Bridget, still seemingly oblivious, continued to try and breastfeed her child.

HER EYES WERE ROLLING IN HER HEAD

The doctor swiftly arrived and saw that Mary's mouth was black. She was struggling to breathe and was barely clinging onto life.

Marks suspiciously like burns on Bridget's breast where she had tried to force Mary to suckle caused the doctor to ask directly if Bridget had poisoned her child. She said all she had done was try to give Mary some castor oil from a bottle that still lay in the child's cot.

The doctor fetched the bottle and could tell straight away that its contents were not castor oil. Bridget Kiernan had fed her baby vitriol. There was nothing the doctor could do to save poor Mary and she died an agonising death within hours.

Bridget was arrested and subsequently charged, despite claiming that she had no idea the white bottle with which she had tried to feed her baby contained the deadly liquid.

An inspection of Mary's cot and her clothes revealed holes where vitriol had splashed from the bottle and burned through the fabric on contact.

Mrs Sparke testified that she sold Bridget a bottle of vitriol the day before Mary's death. People who knew her said Bridget always talked of running away and starting a new life.

Her claims of ignorance fell on deaf ears and she was sentenced to be executed. A public outcry saw a stay of execution granted by order of Queen Victoria. Instead, Bridget spent the rest of her life behind bars in the prison at Dundee's Town House.

SOLD BRIDGET A **BOTTLE** OF **VITRIOL**

BRIDGET KIERNAN

$$HO - \overset{\overset{O}{\|}}{\underset{\underset{O}{\|}}{S}} - OH$$

VITRIOL IS ALSO KNOWN AS SULFURIC ACID

PLAYFAIR
CLOSE, HAWKHILL
The Scene of the Crime

On Saturday 19th October 1872, **Peter Anderson** was charged with throwing vitriol at his wife in Dundee. She completely lost **her sight** and hearing from the attack. He was jailed for five years after pleading guilty, his conduct excusing him of a harsher sentence because of his wife's admitted infidelity!

"She got more than a penny's worth, but her bottle was dirty and I did not take it out again. I put a label on the bottle marked "poison" in printed characters...The vitriol changed colour when I put it into the bottle...there had been oil in the bottle, and hence the change."

Mrs Sparke, who served Bridget vitriol in her brother-in-law Mr Laird's druggist shop.

IT WASN'T UNTIL 1825 THAT THROWING VITRIOL WAS MADE A CAPITAL CRIME

 1868

THE PHARMACY ACT (1868) INTRODUCED SALES RESTRICTIONS AND STRICTER LABELLING OF CHEMICALS

8TH CENTURY

The process of making a concentrated acid from sulfur minerals was discovered by alchemist Jabir ibn Hayyan, whose works include the oldest known systematic classification of chemical substances. He is known as the father of chemistry...but was he even a real person? Many modern scholars seem doubtful. He is noted as dying sometime around 806 - 816 AD.

SULFUR OR SULPHUR?
Sulfur is primarily an American spelling whereas in the UK we use "sulphur"...but the spelling "sulfur" is becoming more commonplace (and it's slightly easier to spell, too!)

"...The child was alive when I was apprehended and I have not seen it since. This morning, one of the policemen told me in prison that the child had died last night a little past six o'clock." (Extract of declaration by Bridget Kiernan, 11th November 1859)

WILLIAM BURY

BEEN SEALED IN THE BOX FOR A WEEK

On 10th February 1889, William Bury reported the death of his wife by suicide, at Bell Street police station. He claimed she had hung herself, and not knowing what to do, had hidden her body inside a wooden box in their squalid flat on Princes Street.

When the police officers arrived at the scene, they found Ellen Bury's body crammed into a tiny wooden crate. Her abdomen had been crudely slashed open; her left leg broken and twisted in an attempt to fit her into the box. She had been secreted there for around a week.

Not believing William's story, he was charged with Ellen's murder. Word spread through the town that the couple had moved just a few weeks earlier from the Whitechapel area of London and that the murder was eerily similar to the Jack the Ripper murders.

With no other Ripper murders occurring since the Burys had left London, newspapers such as The Aberdeen Evening Express and Shields Daily Gazette, exclaimed "JACK THE RIPPER IS IN DUNDEE", and "A WOMAN "WHITECHAPELLED" IN DUNDEE".

There was no evidence against him for any of the Whitechapel murders; William was only on trial for the murder of his wife.

It was clear to the medical examiners that Ellen Bury had most certainly not hanged herself. Marks on her body indicated a struggle.

William pleaded not guilty but with a number of character witnesses testifying to his harsh and often terrifying treatment of his wife over the years, as well as the opinion of the medical examiners who looked over Ellen's body, the jury returned a guilty verdict.

They did however ask for clemency from execution but the Judge refused, the sentence imposed being death by hanging.

William was executed on 24th April 1889 in the grounds of Dundee Prison on Bell Street, where he was also buried.

Officers from Scotland Yard did speak to him, but did not peg him as a credible Ripper suspect. His executioner, James Berry, however, thought the complete opposite.

Regardless, William Bury was dead, and with his passing, so did almost all association linking him with the Whitechapel murders. Unbeknown to us at the time, this was also to be the last execution in Dundee.

HARSH AND
OFTEN **TERRIFYING**
TREATMENT

WILLIAM BURY

28TH MARCH 1889
The date William Bury's trial was seen before **Lord Young** in Dundee.

AN ORPHAN FROM A **YOUNG** AGE
William's father died in an accident 6 weeks before his son's birth. His mother was admitted to a Lunatic asylum and gave birth to him there 3 weeks later. She died there in 1860 aged 33, 2 months before William's 4th birthday.

Jack the Ripper was the name given to the murderer of at least five women, all prostitutes, in or around the Whitechapel district of London's East End, between August and November 1888 (putting the murderer and William Bury in the same time and place). The case is one of the most famous unsolved murders in history.

"**YESTERDAY'S** PROCEEDINGS AMOUNTED TO NOTHING **LESS** THAN COLD BLOODED **MURDER**."
THE DUNDEE COURIER, 1889 on William Bury's execution.

"JACK **RIPPER** **IS IN** THIS SELLER" [SIC]
POORLY-SPELLED CHALK ETCHING FOUND OUTSIDE THE BURY'S HOME

WILLIAM HENRY BURY
BORN: 25TH MAY 1859
DIED: 24TH APRIL 1889

THE LAST EXECUTION
Bury's execution may have been the last execution in Dundee but it was by no means public. He was executed in front of a handful of officials.

DR TEMPLEMAN AND DR STALKER PERFORMED ELLEN'S POST MORTEM ON 11TH FEBRUARY 1889

William and Ellen Bury briefly stayed at 43 UNION STREET before moving to 113 PRINCES STREET

• • • • • • • • •

MARJORIE SMITH
William and Ellen's neighbour claimed that Ellen Bury had told her "the Ripper is quiet now" during a conversation with her on 30th January 1889.

William Bury's headstone, inscribed with only his initials WHB (William Henry Bury) is held by The McManus in their Collections Unit on Barrack Street.

TIMELINE OF **EXECUTIONS** IN **DUNDEE** IN THE **1800's**

12th JUNE 1801

John Watt was executed at the Town House for theft by housebreaking.

2nd JUNE 1826

David Balfour was executed at the Town House for the murder of his estranged wife Margaret.

30th MAY 1835

Mark Devlin was executed at the Town House for the rape of a 15 year old girl.

25th MARCH 1839

Arthur Wood was executed in the Dundee Prison grounds (Bell Street) for the murder of his son John.

5th OCTOBER 1847

Thomas Leith was executed in the Dundee Prison grounds (Bell Street) for the murder of his estranged wife Ann.

24th APRIL 1889

William Bury was executed privately in the Dundee Prison grounds (Bell Street) for the murder of his wife Ellen.

MARK DEVLIN

A CAPITAL CRIME REQUIRING A HIGH COURT TRIAL

In 1835, 26 year old Mark Devlin was arrested and charged with reset (possessing stolen goods) following a robbery in the Hawkhill area of Dundee, along with two other men, James Leys and David Walker.

While in custody however, he was charged with a much more serious crime, the rape of 15 year old Ann McLachlan at the back of the Law, a capital crime requiring a High Court trial.

In Edinburgh, he pleaded his innocence to the court but was found guilty and sentenced to be hanged in Dundee on 30th May 1835.

Not many executions took place in Dundee and our gallows were decades old, so a new scaffold was built and erected the night before the execution.

The builders were so noisy, they woke him up. Despite hearing the sound of his own death trap being built, he fell back asleep and slept through the rest of the construction.

The execution went ahead smoothly, with a near-silent crowd watching as he died and was cut down. There was one odd thing about this textbook hanging, however; the executioner wore a hood.

The execution of Mark Devlin was the only public execution in Dundee during the 1800's where the hangman wore a hood. It was also the last execution for rape in Scotland.

Rumours swirled about the identity of the masked executioner, with many saying that a local volunteer was surely behind the hood, trying to conceal himself.

Travelling salesman James Livingstone found himself accused by the public of being the executioner. He had to have a letter published in the Dundee Advertiser, signed by the Forfar Magistrates as proof of his whereabouts on the day.

It didn't really stop the gossip, but to this day, the identity of the masked executioner remains a mystery.

THE **LAST** EXECUTION FOR **RAPE** IN **SCOTLAND**

MARK DEVLIN

A TRIPLE EXECUTION

In October 1817, three men were executed in Greenock following their conviction for breaking into the house of Robert Morris. They bound him, stole a quantity of money and clothes and raped his sister-in-law and a female servant. The execution of three people at the same time for the same crime was almost unheard of in Scotland at the time.

WE DIDN'T HAVE OUR OWN TOWN EXECUTIONER IN DUNDEE IN THE 1800's. IT IS BELIEVED THAT A HIRED EXECUTIONER DIDN'T APPEAR ON THE DAY OF MARK DEVLIN'S EXECUTION AND THIS IS WHY A 'LOCAL' MAY HAVE STEPPED IN BUT INSISTED ON WEARING A MASK

When we picture a hangman, usually one of the first things we think of is his infamous hood. In Scotland, hangmen usually didn't cover their faces with hoods or try to conceal their identity in any way. Who would want to mess with the hangman - he knows how to snap your neck!

HANGING WAS INTRODUCED TO **BRITAIN** BY THE **GERMANIC ANGLO-SAXON** TRIBES AROUND THE **5TH** CENTURY

14 THE **NUMBER** OF **POLICE OFFICERS** IN DUNDEE IN 1835

DIDN'T ALWAYS GO AS PLANNED

In a "textbook" situation, hanging results in the neck being broken, severing the spine and dropping blood pressure down to 0 in about 1 second. The victim loses consciousness but brain death does not occur for several minutes and full death can take up to 20 minutes after the neck has broken. It doesn't always go to plan however, with horror stories of broken ropes leading to secondary hangings, slow, horrifying deaths due to incorrect knot placement, inexperienced executioners, misjudged rope lengths and full decapitations. Turns out it's not that easy to be a hangman!

JAMES AND DAVID MAY HAVE ESCAPED THE HANGMAN'S NOOSE, BUT THEY DID NOT ESCAPE PUNISHMENT AND WERE TRANSPORTED FOR THEIR CRIMES (WHICH WAS A CHEAP AND EASY WAY TO GET CRIMINALS OUT OF YOUR TOWN)

WASN'T AFRAID TO FLASH AN AN ANKLE

Miss Jean Milne was called an eccentric character by many; a rich and single heiress in her late sixties who travelled around the country and Europe.

She lived alone in a large house in the North-West area of Broughty Ferry and was somewhat of a recluse when there, in stark contrast to her out-of-town social life. She wasn't afraid to flash an ankle in a time when ladies flashing their ankles was frowned upon!

She was found brutally murdered in her home on 3rd November 1912, her limbs bound with rope. She had been beaten repeatedly around the head with a poker as well as stabbed several times with a carving fork, both found lying nearby.

Blood splattered the walls and soaked through the floor where her body had lain for some weeks before being discovered.

The reason she had lain so long and why nobody had missed her was because they had presumed she was on one of her many jaunts.

Nothing was missing or appeared stolen, despite there being plenty of valuables and jewellery around. With no sign of forced entry, it was assumed that either the killer must have known her personally or had snuck into her home while she was out in the garden and had hidden in wait to strike.

Not many knew about her comings and goings, although neighbours said they had spotted a man in the area around the time of her death. Rumours ran wild about who the killer could be, with Miss Milne's personal life coming under intense police as well as public scrutiny.

Police looked into all her known associates, including gentlemen she had spent time with whilst travelling, but everyone had verifiable alibis and/or credible witnesses.

No one knew why someone would want to murder such a seemingly innocent woman, especially if monetary gain wasn't the motivation.

The police were stumped, and despite bringing in outside experts, this case remains one of Scotland's oldest unsolved murders.

HIDDEN
IN WAIT
TO STRIKE

JEAN MILNE

£1,000 **JEAN MILNE'S** ANNUAL INCOME; THE **EQUIVALENT** OF OVER **£110,000** A YEAR IN 2020

DETECTIVE LIEUTENANT JOHN TRENCH

Was drafted in from Glasgow to help with the case based on his success in solving an eerily similar case in Glasgow involving a wealthy murdered widow.

THE STAGES OF HUMAN DECOMPOSITION

AUTOLYSIS
The body's membranes release enzymes that begin eating cells from the inside out. Rigor mortis will cause muscle stiffening and blisters may appear on the body.

BLOAT
Leaked enzymes get gassy inside the body and can swell a corpse up to twice its normal size. The body begins to rot and decay as the gases leak out. This is called putrefaction.

ACTIVE DECAY
Soft tissues have become so decayed they are now liquefied and are being released through any orifices in the corpse, including tears in the skin due to swelling and rotting.

SKELETONISATION
Any last remaining soft tissues of the corpse have completely decayed or dried to the point that the skeleton is exposed.

THE UK'S "OLDEST" UNSOLVED MURDER MYSTERY

The Mount Stewart Murder, 1866.

Janet Rogers, a domestic servant, was found dead in a pool of blood at her brother's Perthshire farmhouse. Her brother William had returned to the farmhouse and upon finding the door locked and no response when he knocked or called, proceeded to climb through a window where he quickly found his sister's body. She had been bludgeoned to death with an axe. A ploughman was initially accused of committing the crime after a botched robbery, but the jury took only 12 minutes to return a verdict of not proven. Nobody else was ever accused, making this case the oldest recorded unsolved murder mystery of any police force in the UK (we are certain there were plenty of unrecorded unsolved murders before the Police Act was established).

ALEXANDER TROUP
Told police that he had seen Miss Jean Milne at her bedroom window on Monday 21st October. Was he mistaken or was there someone in her home 5 days after her murder whilst her body was still lying at the bottom of the stairs?

"**EVERYTHING** POINTS TO THE MURDER HAVING BEEN **COMMITTED** EITHER ON 15TH OR 16TH OCTOBER 1912"
EXTRACT FROM POLICE REPORT ON JEAN MILNE

69 JEAN MILNE'S **AGE**

Restless & Unruly

Times have changed but one thing has remained a constant and that is humanities restless and unruly nature. Some people love to cause fights and some love to fight for a cause. In Dundee, blood has been spilled through siege, war, famine, poverty, politics or sometimes for no good reason at all.

THE RIOT ACT

A slightly snappier name for the much wordier 1714 "Act for Preventing Tumults and Riotous Assemblies, and for the more speedy and effectual Punishing the Rioters", which came into effect in August 1715 after a period of riots in the early 1700's. It had to be read aloud by a "head official" of the town, directly to the crowds and had to follow this exact wording or be deemed entirely invalid, forcing the reader to start again:

"Our sovereign lord the King chargeth and commandeth all persons, being assembled, immediately to disperse themselves, and peaceably to depart to their habitations, or to their lawful business, upon the pains contained in the act made in the first year of King George, for preventing tumults and riotous assemblies. God save the King."

If a group of people failed to disperse within the hour, local authorities could use force to disperse them. Anyone assisting with the dispersal was explicitly absolved of any legal consequences in the event of someone being injured or killed during the process.

KNOW YOUR RIOTS
4 TYPES OF RIOT
COMMUNAL RIOT
COMMODITY RIOT
PROTEST RIOT
REVELRY / CELEBRATION RIOT
ENCYCLOPEDIA.COM

A RIOT is a form of CIVIL DISORDER commonly characterised by a group lashing out in a VIOLENT public disturbance against authority, property, or people. Riots typically involve DESTRUCTION of property.

TOP 10 SCOTTISH RIOTS
COMPILED BY SCOTTISHFIELD.CO.UK

Battle of George Square, GLASGOW, 1919
King's Birthday Riots, EDINBURGH, 1792
Tron Riot, EDINBURGH, 1811/12
Royal High School Riot, EDINBURGH, 1595
Galloway Leveller's Uprising, KIRKCUDBRIGHT, 1724

Siege of St Andrews Castle, ST ANDREWS, 1546
The Massacre of the Rosses, STRATHCARRON, 1854
Porteous Riots, EDINBURGH, 1736
Battle of Bonnymuir, GREENOCK, 1820
Handloom Weaver's Riot, GLASGOW, 1787

THE TREE OF LIBERTY

In the early 1790's, a group of revolutionary supporters called the Friends of Liberty, having been bolstered by recent rumblings across the globe, took it upon themselves to plant a tree in honour of the French Revolution that was happening at the time and all that it stood for.

A fir tree was planted in the centre of town as a symbol of freedom, equality and liberty...until someone stole it and it all kicked off. Despite widely communicated threats of violence and uprising if the tree was not returned, the tree never reappeared.

OUT OF HAND **A LITTLE** TOO QUICKLY

News spread like wildfire that hundreds of people, many more than there were supporters of the Friends of Liberty had descended on the town centre. As bonfires were lit and the drinks were flowing, things got out of hand a little too quickly.

Property not belonging to the mob was destroyed and burned to keep the fires going and the group's tempers flared. They had decided they wanted a new tree and knew exactly where they could get one.

The Belmont estate (currently the site of DJCAD) had recently been built for Thomas Bell and his family; a large home with newly planted gardens. Dozens of men carrying torches, spades and goodness knows what else all marched up to the property, scaled the boundary wall and stole an ash tree from the grounds.

Causing untold damage to property and buildings on their way back to the centre of town, they planted their stolen tree and partied into the night as town officials cowered in fear and sent for backup.

PARTIED INTO THE **NIGHT**

As daylight dawned and headaches were many, the presence of guards in the town stopped another riot from happening when the Friends of Liberty saw that their tree had been jailed in the 'thief's hole' of the Town House.

Making a mockery of their symbol and what it stood for by jailing the tree, the officials had the last laugh. Laws in place against so much as making a leaflet deemed as anti-government saw some members arrested and transported for up to 14 years for their crimes.

THE TREE OF LIBERTY

During a period of the French Revolution known as 'The Terror' (June 1793 to July 1794), 40,000 people were killed in France. 17,000 of these were executed by guillotine.

THOMAS FYSHE PALMER

SURPRIZE

Muir, Palmer, Skirving and Margarot, together with Margarot's wife and Palmer's friend James Ellis were all taken to Australia aboard the same convict ship, the Surprize, which set sail on 2 May 1794. Rather than supporting each other, the radicals fell out when Palmer and Skirving were accused by the captain of conspiring to incite a mutiny and Palmer accused Margarot of spreading rumours.

A Unitarian minister and member of the Friends of Liberty in Dundee. Sentenced to 7 years transportation for printing and distributing a leaflet. He died of dysentery in 1802 on the island of Guam on route home after the completion of his sentence.

THE SEVEN SCOTTISH MARTYRS

The 7 political reformers sentenced for sedition and treason between 1792 and 1798 were not all from one group but were all influenced by the French revolutionaries.
William Skirving, Thomas Muir, Thomas Fyshe Palmer, Maurice Margarot, Joseph Gerrald and George Mealmaker were transported to Botany Bay.
The seventh martyr, Robert Watt, was hanged and beheaded for treason in October 1794.
In total, the 6 other martyrs were sentenced to 77 years between them for speaking out against the government.

WHAT HAPPENED TO THE TREE?

The second tree of liberty (because we don't know what happened to the original stolen fir tree) was re-planted at the Belmont estate. It stayed there for over a hundred years but it was cut down due to road widening in the 1930's. A new version of the tree was planted in 1986 but it was also removed in 2012 as it never really thrived and a new entrance for the art college was being built.

23 HEIGHT IN METRES OF THE AVERAGE ASH TREE

ASH TREES CAN LIVE FOR AROUND 200 - 300 YEARS, WITH SOME LIVING AS LONG AS 400 YEARS

FANNY WRIGHT (1795 - 1852)
Daughter of Friends of Liberty member James Wright, she clearly took after her father even though he died when she was just 2 years old. Fanny (Frances) went on to become an outspoken feminist and social reformer.

THE SIEGE OF 1651

On 1st September 1651, General George Monck, Commander-in-chief to Oliver Cromwell, stormed the town of Dundee with bloody consequences.

Dundee was completely walled-in at that time and was a rich and thriving community. It was home to the largest gold depository in Scotland, with the wealth of many viscounts and earls nestled within the safety of its confines.

LICENCE TO LOOT AND PILLAGE THE BESIEGED TOWN

Upon forcing entry, Monck promised his troops 24 hours free licence to loot and pillage the besieged town. Monck quickly lost control of his troops and as a result, the killing and looting went on for 3 days or more.

The town's defenders were rounded up and massacred without mercy. The town was pillaged and was set on fire, women raped and men, women and children put to the sword in a killing frenzy.

The Governor of Dundee, Robert Lumsden gathered his remaining men to make a last stand in the tower of St. Mary's (the Old Steeple).

They barricaded the only doorway and the thick walls of the tower provided a safe place to defend. Monck had a plan to get them out and ordered fires to be set at the base of the tower. Damp straw and willow bark were lit which produced a lot of smoke. As the tower filled, Lumsden and his men had no choice but to surrender or they would die from smoke inhalation.

Governor Lumsden was not spared upon his surrender. He was shot, beheaded and had his head placed on a spike which was then displayed from the parapets of the tower.

THE **TOWER** FILLED WITH **THICK** SMOKE

The troops pillaged everything of value they could find and a fleet of ships was required to carry their vast haul out of the ruined town. It's estimated the total value could have been up to £2 billion. Some say the once wealthy and prosperous town never fully recovered.

Today we unknowingly walk over the bodies of those fallen during this bloody siege, buried in mass graves underneath the streets of the city centre.

THE SIEGE OF 1651

WHY WAS DUNDEE ATTACKED?

Oliver Cromwell was one of the people who signed for Charles I's execution in 1649 and brutally crushed any remaining royalist support in Ireland. He then set his sights on Scotland, as we had declared Charles II King. Dundee was a royalist town and General Monck was sent to capture it.

A summons was sent to Governor Lumsden on 26th August, inviting Lumsden to surrender the town on Monck's terms. With the walls of the town being recently fortified, Lumsden was confident. He not only refused to surrender but he suggested to Monck his army should lay down THEIR arms!

THE RULES OF ENGAGEMENT

The rules of war were harsh. If a garrison surrendered immediately on summons, they would be treated well and get good terms of surrender. If they held out for a while, but eventually surrendered they could still get reasonable terms. If the stronghold had to be taken by force, it was up to the victor to decide their fate.

Storming a town or fortified stronghold was difficult and usually involved a lot of death on the invading army's side. The soldiers needed some kind of incentive to fight, and 24 hours free licence to rape and pillage a town without discretion was enough motivation for most.

160 HEIGHT IN FEET OF THE OLD STEEPLE OF ST MARY'S
SCOTLAND'S TALLEST MEDIEVAL TOWER
160FT EQUALS 48.77 METRES

HOW MANY PEOPLE DIED DURING THE SIEGE?

Some have suggested up to 2,000 people died overall; other reports show 500 soldiers dead, and over 80 townspeople killed during the initial siege itself. The number is likely somewhere in the middle.

REST IN PIECES

Just over two years after his peacefully natural death on 30th January 1661 (the 12th anniversary of the execution of Charles I) Oliver Cromwell's body was exhumed by royalist supporters from its resting place at Westminster Abbey and beheaded. His head was displayed atop a pole outside Westminster Hall for more than 20 years.

PARTY POOPER

Cromwell is often described as a 'killjoy' because he passed laws forbidding dancing, Christmas, drunkenness and the theatre. He wanted people to focus thoughtfully on the word of God at all times.

MONCK'S DIARY OF THE SIEGE OF DUNDEE

Selected quotes from 'A Narrative or Diary of the Proceedings of the
Forces under Lt. General Monck - generalmonck.com

"Sept. 1. About 4 o'clock in the morning our great guns began to play before Dundee round about the line. The enemy for two or three hours answered us gun for gun, besides small shot from their works, til such time as large breaches were made in two of their most considerable forts...

Three hundred horse and dragoons, being eleven of [each?] troop, were appointed to fall on with the foot with sword and pistol. Our men were drawn forth in ambuscades by daybreak to fall upon when breaches were made, and with them 200 seamen...and 400 horse...

Capt. Hart led on the forlorn of Lt. General Monck's regiment on the west side, Major Robinson the horse, and Col. Ashfeild's [sic] regiment went on the east side. Capt. Ely led on the Pioneers [engineer troops] who made way for the horse [through the breaches], and the Lt. General went in person. Our word was "God with us," and the sign a white cloth or shirt hanging out behind...

About 11 o'clock the signal was given, and breaches being made into the enemy's forts on the east and west sides of the town, our men entered, and after about half an hour of hot dispute, diverse of the enemy retreated to the church and steeple, and amongst the rest the Governor, who was killed with between four and five hundred soldiers and townsmen...

There was killed of ours Capt. Hart and about 20 soldiers, and as many wounded.

When our men got to the marketplace they gave quarter, and took about 500 prisoners, and amongst the rest Col. Coningham, Governor of Sterling, who was in the town....

The soldiers had the plunder of the town for all that day and night, and had very large prize, many inhabitants of Edinburgh and other places having sent their ware and gear thither.

By the best testimony we could get, the townspeople were most obstinate against a rendition on terms, being confident of their own works and strength, having formerly beat out Montrosse [sic], but they have now most suffered for it, and paid dearly for their contempt."

MAG GOW

A repeat offender of the 1800's, fish-seller Mag Gow racked up an obscene number of court appearances over the years for drunkenness, breach of the peace and, on occasion, assault.

When drunk (which was often), she would break out into wild, outrageous fits which attracted crowds in the streets. Mag was stuck in a vicious cycle of drinking to provide solace for her troubles. With a limited social circle, she had befriended other known habitual drinkers, who only fed into her addiction.

STUCK IN A VICIOUS CYCLE OF DRINKING

She was a target for wisecracking and unruly boys who would hound and harass her everywhere she went. They'd take her fish basket and empty it onto the streets and cover her face and clothes with horse manure.

Even as she told the court of how the 'laddies' had taken her fish, the room roared with laughter, everyone enjoying the spectacle of Mag Gow in court and her 'crazy stories'.

On a Friday morning at the end of June 1877, Mag was released from her 60 day stint in jail (having being sent to prison the February prior and then again at the end of April). By 1am on Saturday morning she was in the streets, practically blind drunk and screaming her head off.

She was dragged back to the police station less than 24 hours after she was released and was sentenced to yet another 60 days.

BLIND **DRUNK** AND SCREAMING HER HEAD **OFF**

It wasn't until she was seen in court again in November of the same year that something changed in Mag's cycle of torment. Doctors were ordered to assess her state of health and declared her insane. Mag found herself sentenced to a stay in the asylum.

Once she had been sober for a while, they'd release her to go back to her life selling fish, but every time they did she was back on the bottle, in the court and returned to the asylum again. When Mag died in 1903, The Courier reported that she held the record of number of criminal convictions of anyone in the city.

MAG GOW

256
NUMBER OF
CONVICTIONS
HELD BY MAG
GOW UPON
HER DEATH

On 28th April 1862, The Courier newspaper had to print an apology to Mag and her father, after he wrote a letter to them regarding a misstatement "conceived to be injurious to the reputation of his daughter."
They had printed she had been convicted 140 times and corrected this as it had only been a measly 104 appearances up until that point!

On 10th May 1866, The Dundee Courier reported that Mag had been found "lying insensibly drunk in Overgate" and had to be "hurled to the Police Office in a barrow."

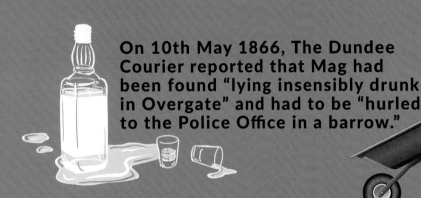

MARY ANN STEWART
Second on the highest female convictions rate list, Mary Ann Stewart's number of convictions in her lifetime was 140.

HER LAST DAY IN COURT

On Saturday 18th May 1889, Mag Gow appeared before the court for the last time, charged with breach of the peace.

She was found drunk, shouting and swearing at the door of a house in Crichton Street and then forcing her way in 'to the annoyance' of the people inside.

As she had previously been staying at the lunatic ward of the Eastern Poorhouse for many years, she was medically examined and immediately sent back there, where it appears she stayed until her death in 1903.

In the late 1870's, the crime of 'shebeening' (selling alcohol without a licence) was a crime committed by more women than men, often landing them with hefty fines or a spell in the gaol.

In the 1840's in Dundee there was **1 PUB** for every **24 FAMILIES**

70
MAG WAS AGED AROUND 70 WHEN SHE DIED

CORONATION DAY RIOT

On Thursday 28th June 1838, an outdoor street party in Dundee to celebrate the coronation of Queen Victoria got a little out of hand.

When the crowds first gathered in the streets that afternoon to celebrate, the atmosphere was full of fun and excitement. However, as the evening wore on, the mood turned.

Some young men who were looking to cause trouble started throwing bits of metal, broken crates and home-made fireworks into the throng. Cheers of celebration were drowned out by cries of pain as thousands of people dived for cover, several hurt and bleeding.

Seeing a rare chance to take part in an evening of wanton destruction, Jonathan Haziel headed a troop of unruly locals to the harbour to steal a boat.

The harbour police descended upon the mob as they were pulling the boat to shore by hand but, vastly outnumbered, they were severely beaten by the angry gang of men. By 9pm, a Dundee man named William Gunn and his friend-in-arms David Lyon led others in lighting fires in the streets.

YOUNG MEN WHO WERE LOOKING TO CAUSE TROUBLE

BECAME AN
UNCONTROLLABLE
INFERNO

Haziel and his gang had reappeared around this time, dragging the boat they had stolen from the harbour. They then lit up a tar barrel, flung it into the boat and hauled it through the High Street to cheers and whoops from the belligerent crowd.

They reached the bottom of Union Street and broke into Scot's Shakespearean Pantheon Theatre. The horde hammered down the doors and dragged furnishings and fittings into the street.

More fires were lit and the loot dumped onto the flames as well as onto the still-burning boat. Suddenly, the tar roof-covering of the Pantheon ignited. In a matter of seconds, flames enveloped the building's wooden frame.

The theatre became an uncontrollable inferno. As the Pantheon burned, the mob scattered and ran. With plenty of witnesses, including several battered police officers, it didn't take long to pinpoint the trio. Lyon, Gunn and Haziel were all arrested, charged and hauled before the court, where they were unanimously found guilty of mobbing, rioting, breach of the peace and malicious mischief.

CORONATION DAY RIOT

Several riots in Dundee, especially in the 1800's, involved dragging a burning boat up the High Street. When the evening wore on and rioters wanted to keep going, they lit bonfires for light and warmth. Boats were handy as they were essentially mobile bonfires until they, too, burned to cinders.

LORD MEDWYN

THE JUDGE IN THIS CASE, WAS BORN IN **1776**. HE WAS APPOINTED SHERIFF DEPUTE OF PERTHSHIRE IN **1807**, LORD OF SESSION IN **1825** AND LORD OF JUSTICIARY IN **1830**. HE DIED IN **1854** AGED **77**

24 MONTHS

Surprisingly, the men received lenient sentences for their crimes, with Haziel sentenced to 8 months in the Dundee Prison on Bell Street.

Gunn received 4 months, and Lyon 12 months; a collective sentence of 24 months for their instrumental involvement in the Coronation Day riot.

5,000 There were so many people still in town from the party in the afternoon, it's hard to say how many people were 'mobbing'. Some reports estimated that almost 5,000 rioters joined.

ROYAL MISHAPS

Queen Victoria's coronation itself didn't exactly go without a hitch. First, the Archbishop put the ring on the wrong finger and it got stuck, then the Bishop of Duran accidentally turned over two pages during the service and had to call the Queen back to do it again. As if this wasn't enough drama, Lord Rolle (who was 82 years old) fell over when ascending the steps towards the new Queen and literally rolled back down them! The whole affair took over 5 hours!

THE EARLIEST HARBOUR IS BELIEVED TO HAVE BEEN AT WHAT IS NOW THE **GELLATLY STREET/SEAGATE JUNCTION**

THE PORT HAD MOVED **WESTWARDS** BY THE **16TH** CENTURY TO ROUGHLY WHERE **WHITEHALL CRESCENT** IS TODAY

MARY BROOKSBANK

Born in an Aberdeen slum in 1897, Mary's family moved to Dundee for a new start when she was just 8 years old. By the time Mary was 11 she was working illegally in one of the city's many jute mills.

Mill conditions were largely appalling; wages were low and the hours were long. At age 14 Mary saw what could happen when workers stood up to their bosses as she watched mill girls marching for, and winning, a 15% pay rise.

WOMEN'S RIGHTS, **EQUALITY AND** WORKERS' RIGHTS

Mary grew up in a world of dust and machinery. Low wages, poor treatment and terrible living conditions pushed her to become an active protestor and organiser.

At 21, she joined the Communist Party fighting for women's rights, equality and workers' rights. Mary wanted to be the voice for so many who felt they couldn't speak out against the terrible working conditions in the mills, or risk losing their jobs.

Not afraid to use her fists as well as her voice, Mary was arrested several times in her life including once for sedition.

DIVING INTO THE BRAWL

She was found guilty of speaking at a Communist Party meeting and encouraging the audience to smash windows and use violence in protest. She also had 3 stints in jail, the longest of which was 3 months for inciting a crowd to riot (sedition) in September 1931.

Over 3 days, thousands of people rioted on the streets of Dundee because of unemployment rates, with constant clashes between police and the mobs. When men were seen fleeing from a fellow protestor who was being beaten by police, Mary shouted 'if the men won't fight then the women will' diving into the brawl.

She was arrested later that day when Constable Finnock saw her trying to rally a section of the women in the crowd. She had a torch in one hand and the leg of a table in the other which she threw at him and then proceeded to hit him with her lit torch.

Mary was blacklisted from all the city's jute mills because of her protesting. They saw her as a trouble maker, but today she is remembered for her poetry and songs and as a champion of workers' rights.

MARY BROOKSBANK

CYCLING DAYS

Mary Brooksbank's first poem 'Cycling Days' was written whilst she was an inmate in **Perth Prison**.

1966 MARY'S WORK IS PUBLISHED FOR THE FIRST TIME

When Mary's family moved to Dundee, they lived at the foot of the **Overgate**, and later **Blackness Road**. She is quoted as saying about her childhood homes "we lost a beautiful baby brother, aged two and a half, a victim of diphtheria. No winder![SIC] The overcrowding was atrocious, as were the toilet facilities, or rather lack of them, for we had one WC between four tenants."

Her songs were political and included topics about life in Dundee's textile mills, women's issues and historic/literary milestones.

100+ Between **1889** and **1914**, over one hundred strike actions were called in Dundee, most of them led by women.

ONE OF TEN CHILDREN

5 of Mary's other 9 siblings sadly didn't make it past infancy. At the time, infant mortality was as high as **30%** in the poorest areas of town.

MARY BROOKSBANK WAS BORN BLIND. SHE RECOVERED HER SIGHT 14 MONTHS AFTER HER BIRTH

THE WALLS OF THE SCOTTISH PARLIAMENT

Lines from her most famous song 'Oh Dear Me' are inscribed on the Canongate Wall of the Scottish Parliament building - the only woman to be quoted on the wall.

Oh, dear me, the world's ill-divided,
Them that work the hardest are aye wi' least provided,
But I maun bide contented, dark days or fine,
But there's no much pleasure livin' affen ten and nine.

Mary Brooksbank (1897 - 1978), Oh Dear Me (The Jute Mill Song)

STOBS FAIR

In the late 1600's, Dundee's most notoriously unruly fair started. Held about a mile and a half outside town at Stobs Muir, it was called, unsurprisingly, Stobs Fair.

It was an agricultural fair, but always attracted crowds, so tents full of booze and entertainment sprung up to cater to them. Bringing people together from all walks of life and letting them get roaring drunk was never going to end well, and Stobs Fair was our annual party of booze, fun and total mayhem.

There were gangs of young lads who had an unusual tradition for closing the fair each year with a battle.

BOOZE, FUN AND TOTAL MAYHEM

They would rain missiles upon the fair-goers - stones, sticks, clods of mud, anything they could get their hands on, causing everyone to run. In the summer of 1809, the 25th Regiment were at Dudhope Castle and were sent to Stobs Fair to recruit.

During the course of their recruitment drive, an argument started up between some of the adolescents and some of the men from the Regiment over who had broken a drum-head.

When the end of fair battle began, the young lads with some local artillerymen were on one side and the 25th Regiment, with their swords and bayonets were on the other.

A volley of missiles aimed directly at the soldiers faces caused them to be enraged and they charged at the Dundee mob as if they were on a real battlefield. The two sides clashed savagely with casualties in both groups.

SKULL CLEFT WITH A SWORD

Some of the soldiers were brutally attacked; two of them beaten unconscious and requiring hospitalisation. One of the Dundee youths had been hit hard on the head with a stone during the melee. He staggered home without seeking help, only to be found dead the following morning.

One of the porters at the fair had his skull cleft with a sword, but luckily survived. Unbelievably, despite the carnage caused, nobody was held to account; it was just expected that this was what happened if you went to Stobs Fair.

STOBS FAIR

DEATH AT THE FAIR

In 1824, there were a few more gangs at Stobs Fair than usual, with fights breaking out all over the place. A group of masons were attacked and beaten so badly that one of them named John Allan was killed by a blow to the head.

THE LAST STOBS FAIR WAS HELD IN 1901

Stobsmuir Park - also known as 'swannie ponds' - is part of where Stobs Muir used to be. The area is also called Stobswell.

40 NUMBER OF YEARS PEACE AT STOBS FAIR AFTER JOHN ALLAN'S DEATH

In 1864 a man was asked by the police to stop performing at the Lady Mary Fair in Dundee. His "act" was to skin rats alive with his teeth before biting their heads off!

The fair moved to Fairmuir in 1830 and none of the previous traditions of fighting and rioting seemed to follow it until 1864 when a drunken battle between Irishmen and local youths broke out. Suddenly, everyone was fighting and the police didn't know what to do as Stobs Fair had remained peaceful since the appointment of official police officers in the town, thanks to the Police Act of 1824. It only calmed down because everyone eventually got tired and went home!

"The fair **concluded** as usual with **much** noise, many **black** eyes and **bloody** noses."

Quote from the Dundee Advertiser, 25th July 1803.

1870 appears to be the last record of major trouble at the fair, resulting in a mob causing masses of damage as they fled from police down the Hilltown. Windows were smashed and broken carts and milk bottles littered the streets alongside hundreds of torn and trampled hats.

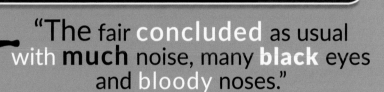

The Supernatural

Regardless of your belief in the supernatural, there have been plenty of strange and mysterious incidents in Dundee which have certainly raised an eyebrow or two. From things that go bump in the night, to ancient serpents, Dundee has seen and been scared of them all.

The ancient Romans believed a ghost could be used to exact revenge on an enemy by scratching a curse on a piece of lead or pottery and placing it into a grave.

PHASMOPHOBIA
THE INTENSE FEAR OF GHOSTS AND THE SUPERNATURAL

The UK is ranked as one of the most haunted places in the world. The first official group formed to investigate paranormal activity was The Society for Psychical Research, founded in London in 1882.

WICCAPHOBIA
THE INTENSE FEAR OF WITCHES AND WITCHCRAFT

The earliest known written magical incantations come from ancient Mesopotamia (modern-day Iraq), inscribed on clay tablets dated to between the 5th and 4th centuries BC.

SHIPS CAN BE GHOSTS, TOO!

Legends such as the 18th century tale of the ghost ship **The Flying Dutchman** or the Spanish ghost ship **The Caleuche**, both said to appear as if from nowhere either carrying or ferrying the dead have spawned tales lasting centuries. However, not every ghost ship is an old wives' tale. Some truly have been deserted, such as the **Mary Celeste**, who was found floating aimlessly in the Atlantic Ocean in 1872 without a crew but with all her cargo intact. Others have ferried the truly dead, such as the **Octavius**, a three-masted schooner found off the coast of **Greenland** by the whaling ship **Herald**. All of the crew of Octavius had died, frozen solid by the icy temperatures. Their captain was found sitting upright and **frozen** at his desk, his logbook open showing a date 13 years prior to their discovery.

SALEM WITCH TRIALS
1692 - 1693, MASSACHUSETTS
OVER **200** PEOPLE ACCUSED
30 FOUND GUILTY
19 HANGED
14 WOMEN, 5 MEN

JANET HORNE

Janet Horne (probably not her real name) was the last person legally executed for witchcraft in the UK. She was stripped naked, smeared with tar and burned in a barrel in her hometown of Dornoch in 1727.

THE GHOST OF BLACKNESS

For almost 10 years, rumours and stories circulated the town about a mysterious phantom stalking the Blackness area of Dundee.

To begin with, that's all they were; just stories, until one night in late 1882 when someone finally came face to face with the elusive Blackness ghost.

Night after night, more sightings were reported until children and adults alike all over the town were close to petrified with fear.

WERE CLOSE TO PETRIFIED WITH FEAR

Its darkened figure was said to be as tall as 2 men and those who saw it said it flitted in and out of the shadows, appearing and disappearing as if manifesting itself from thin air.

The hauntings continued throughout the end of 1882 and into the start of 1883, showing no signs of slowing down and turning both believers and sceptics into quivering wrecks.

Things eventually came to a head when an ex-policeman took on the apparition one evening after being alerted to its presence in the Blackness Quarry area where he lived.

Confirming that the apparition was indeed as tall as two men, he also said it didn't seem to like the look of the iron poker he was brandishing as he charged towards it shouting threats of violence.

ADMINISTER
SOME MOB
JUSTICE

After a quick chase, the phantom leapt over the edge of the quarry and into the darkness, eluding the ex-officer and his iron poker.

Emboldened by this, crowds gathered for weeks afterwards hoping to catch sight of the apparition and administer some mob justice. However, with no sightings and the days dragging on, crowds of hundreds became tens, then dwindled away completely.

The Blackness ghost was never seen again. Perhaps it had been upstaged by another entity which rocked the town at the same time, which we'll get to later.

THE GHOST OF BLACKNESS

READ ALL ABOUT IT

SOME GHASTLY HEADLINES OF THE TIMES

THE DUNDEE ADVERTISER
28TH FEBRUARY 1867

A FUNNY GHOST STORY

THE DUNDEE COURIER AND ARGUS
17TH MAY 1869

EXTRAORDINARY GHOST STORY IN DUNDEE

THE DUNDEE COURIER AND ARGUS
22ND JUNE 1869

A GHOST IN LOGIE KIRKYARD

THE PEOPLE'S JOURNAL
5TH AUGUST 1871

THE GHOST OF THE CHAPELSHADE

THE DUNDEE COURIER AND ARGUS
3RD JULY 1872

EXTRAORDINARY GHOST STORY IN DUNDEE

THE DUNDEE COURIER AND ARGUS
28TH DECEMBER 1875

MIDNIGHT APPARITION IN DUNDEE

THE DUNDEE COURIER AND ARGUS
16TH JANUARY 1883

THE GHOST OF BLACKNESS QUARRY A BLACK APPARITION IN DUNDEE

THE DUNDEE COURIER AND ARGUS
6TH FEBRUARY 1883

A GHOST AT LARGE IN DUNDEE ALLEGED SERIOUS RESULTS

THE EVENING POST
22ND DECEMBER 1900

LOCHEE'S GHOST AND THE FAIR MAID

THE COURIER AND ADVERTISER
28TH SEPTEMBER 1927

5000 HUNT DUNDEE "GHOSTS" EVENING SEARCH AT CRAIGIE QUARRIES

THE COURIER AND ADVERTISER
24TH FEBRUARY 1930

GHOSTLY VISITANT TO THE CARSE

THE COURIER AND ADVERTISER
5TH SEPTEMBER 1945

GHOST WALKS BRIDGE "THE WHITE LADY OF COFFIN MILL"

THE COURIER AND ADVERTISER
11TH MARCH 1932

YOUNG MEN GIVE CHASE TO DUNDEE "GHOST"

HELEN DUNCAN

SHE **SAT** WITH CLIENTS AND **COMMUNED** WITH THE DEAD

Victoria Helen McFarlane was born in Callander in 1897. Her childhood "quirks" of talking in multiple tongues, correctly foretelling dark prophecies and knowing information she could not possibly know were something her parents hoped and prayed she would grow out of.

School was a nightmare for her and as she grew, her reputation made her unable to get a job in her hometown because almost everyone was scared to be associated with her.

She found her way to Dundee, gaining employment and, by 1916, a husband, Henry Duncan whom she bore 6 children. He knew of her abilities and encouraged her to make money from her talent.

Helen's reputation as a spiritual medium grew, gaining her much popularity and scrutiny. Nightly, she sat with clients and communed with the dead, producing ectoplasmic forms from her body.

In 1931, a series of tests performed on Helen Duncan proved to be a chaotic affair, pouring more scorn and doubt on her abilities.

Her confidence grew over the years as her star continued to rise. At an Edinburgh séance in 1941, she revealed classified information about the sinking of the battleship HMS Hood, of which several of the crew were from Dundee. She did it again later the same year with the sinking of the HMS Barham.

In 1944, with the Navy desperate to secure a conviction against her, she once again stood trial, but under a centuries-old, antiquated law; the Witchcraft Act of 1735. The case was weak at best and constantly interrupted by air raids (it happened during WWII). Even Winston Churchill waded in to comment on the "tomfoolery" of the situation.

Despite all of this, she was found guilty and sentenced to 9 months in Holloway Prison where she served 6. Her final séance was in Nottingham in 1956 and was interrupted by a police raid. Some officers then committed what is said to be a 'cardinal sin' during a séance; they shone their torches upon her.

A medium should not be touched or have strong lights shone upon them when in a trance. Helen's screams filled the room. She was rushed to hospital with second-degree burns on her body which became septic and killed her in a matter of weeks.

HELEN'S SCREAMS FILLED THE ROOM

HELEN DUNCAN

EXTRACT OF A REPORT WRITTEN BY PSYCHICAL RESEARCHER HARRY PRICE, WHO PERFORMED TESTS ON HELEN DUNCAN UNDER "CONTROLLED" LABORATORY CONDITIONS IN 1931

"At the conclusion of the fourth seance we led the medium to a settee and called for the apparatus. At the sight of it, the lady promptly went into a trance. She recovered, but refused to be X-rayed. Her husband went up to her and told her it was painless. She jumped up and gave him a smashing blow on the face which sent him reeling. Then she went for Dr. William Brown who was present. He dodged the blow. Mrs. Duncan, without the slightest warning, dashed out into the street, had an attack of hysteria and began to tear her seance garment to pieces. She clutched the railings and screamed and screamed. Her husband tried to pacify her. It was useless. I leave the reader to visualize the scene. A seventeen-stone woman, clad in black sateen tights, locked to the railings, screaming at the top of her voice. A crowd collected and the police arrived. The medical men with us explained the position and prevented them from fetching the ambulance. We got her back into the Laboratory and at once she demanded to be X-rayed. In reply, Dr. William Brown turned to Mr. Duncan and asked him to turn out his pockets. He refused and would not allow us to search him. There is no question that his wife had passed him the cheese-cloth in the street. However, they gave us another seance and the "control' said we could cut off a piece of "teleplasm" when it appeared. The sight of half-a-dozen men, each with a pair of scissors waiting for the word, was amusing. It came and we all jumped. One of the doctors got hold of the stuff and secured a piece. The medium screamed and the rest of the "teleplasm" went down her throat. This time it wasn't cheese-cloth. It proved to be paper, soaked in white of egg, and folded into a flattened tube... Could anything be more infantile than a group of grown-up men wasting time, money, and energy on the antics of a fat female crook."

7 THE NUMBER OF CHARGES FACED BY HELEN DUNCAN

2 counts of conspiracy to contravene the Witchcraft Act, 2 of obtaining money by false pretences and 3 of the common law offence of public mischief.

59 Helen Duncan's age when she died on 6th December 1956

PEGGY THE NAME OF HELEN'S SPIRIT GUIDE

THE WITCHCRAFT ACT 1735

outlawed the hunting and execution of witches by making it a crime for a person to claim that any human being had magical powers, was guilty of practicing witchcraft and could summon spirits and demons. By claiming to be a spiritual medium, Helen Duncan effectively broke this law and was one of the last people to be convicted under it (Jane Yorke of London was convicted later in the same year as Helen Duncan). The law was repealed, to be replaced with the 1951 Fraudulent Mediums Act.

THE NINE MAIDENS

This legend has its origins in Pictish times, perhaps sometime between the 6th to the 9th centuries and concerns a farmer and his 9 daughters who lived in Pitempton, on the outskirts of Dundee.

After a strenuous morning tending the land, he sent one of his daughters to a nearby well to fetch water. When she didn't return, he sent another and then another until he had sent all of his 9 daughters to the well, with nobody returning.

MOST HORRIFIC SIGHT THAT COULD BEFALL A FATHER

Upon the last daughter's failure to return, he eventually made his own way to the well only to be met with the most horrific sight that could befall a father.

Strewn by the well were the bodies of his 9 daughters. The farmer saw that a giant serpent lay coiled around some of the crushed and blood-soaked bodies, basking in the sun.

Undoubtedly trying his best to disguise his sheer horror and fright, he retreated to raise the alarm. A mob soon gathered to slay the serpent, led by a young man called Martin, who was alleged to have been the lover of one of the maidens.

With the help of the angry mob, Martin engaged the murderous creature. Having been extremely hurt in the initial encounter and perhaps sensing it was no match for the mob, it fled north towards Baldragon Moss.

It was then said to have been chased towards the area we now know as Strathmartine (once called Strikemartin) for a final showdown. The mob chanted "strike, Martin" as he dealt the killing blow. In its final moments of life, the serpent retreated and died in an area where a Pictish stone now stands.

It was later alleged that a local minister had declared that the maidens were eaten by the serpent for the crime of dancing on a Sunday!

The fateful well was on the south side of the Dichty Burn and was called the Nine Maidens Well. The Pictish stone is said to depict this final encounter between Martin and the serpent. A dragon statue in Dundee's High Street also serves as a more recent reminder of the centuries-old tale.

THE **CRIME** OF DANCING ON A **SUNDAY**

THE NINE MAIDENS

WHO WERE THE PICTS?

The Picts were a group of Celtic-speaking peoples who lived in PICTLAND (what is today eastern and northern Scotland) during the Late British Iron Age and Early Medieval periods.

The term 'Pict' was not the name of the group of peoples themselves, but the name given to them by the Romans, taken to mean "painted" people. Part of their custom was to adorn their bodies with pictorial and decorative tattoos, hence the name.

 9 The number 9 has significant spiritual meaning in many faiths across the world.

BALLUDERON STONE

More commonly known as Martin's Stane (or Stone), the stone is a class II Pictish cross slab dating from around the 6th to 9th centuries. It is made of old red sandstone, carved with men on horses and a serpent, amongst other designs and is said to have been inspired by the tale of Martin, the murderous serpent and the ill-fated 9 maidens of Pitempton.

56.5261°N 3.0179°W
MAP COORDINATES TO MARTIN'S STANE

18TH JULY
FEAST DAY OF THE NINE MAIDENS

DONALD OF OGILVIE

An 8th century Scottish saint who lived in what is now the area of Angus. When his wife died, he and his 9 daughters lived a monastic life. Upon his death, they entered a monastery in Abernethy. They are known as the Nine Maidens or the Nine Holy Virgins. Churches all over Scotland were dedicated to the Nine Maidens and they even have their own Feast Day. St Donald's Feast Day is 15th July, just before his daughters'.

By the beginning of the Middle Ages, Scotland didn't have people called "Picts" anymore. Under the control of King Kenneth MacAlpin, Scotland became a fairly united realm. It would seem that the 'merger' simply absorbed the Picts but legend has it that Kenneth and his men massacred all the Pictish nobles at a banquet and then took power for themselves!

AD 839 YEAR THE VIKINGS MASSACRED THE REMAINING PICTISH ROYAL FAMILY

THE NORSE WATCHER-GOD **HEIMDALLR** WAS SAID TO HAVE BEEN BORN OF NINE MOTHERS

EXECUTION OF DAVID BALFOUR

THE CROWDS CAME IN THEIR THOUSANDS

David Balfour's execution should have gone without a hitch. Despite claims of mental delusion, Balfour was found guilty of the murder of his estranged wife Margaret in her father Robert Clark's Murraygate home on 21st December 1825.

He was sentenced to be executed on 2nd June of the following year. It had been almost 25 years to the day since Dundee had last witnessed a public execution, and the crowds came in their thousands.

Using the quarter of a century old gallows last used on John Watt, Balfour stepped onto the platform erected outside the guildry hall window of the Town House and gave his final speech.

When his speech finished and the Rev Murray started to pray, the sound of horses and coaches began emanating loudly from within the crowd.

Confused at the noise, the crowds began to part and get agitated, but nobody could see the horses or the coaches. The crowd became panicked and started to run.

There were so many people in the heaving throng that some were trampled underfoot, mostly women and children. Fearing a rush or some kind of attempt to save Balfour, the Town House doors were swiftly bolted shut.

Later, reports in the newspapers claimed that the doors to the Town House were also forcibly pushed and banged upon by an unseen force.

Rev Murray continued his prayer as the mysterious horse and carriage sound emanated once again, causing another brief round of confusion and panic in the crowd. Undeterred by the 'spectral noises', Balfour's execution went ahead.

Around 2:50pm that Friday afternoon, David Balfour was hanged in front of a mainly silent crowd. With Balfour's passing, the noise of the phantom horse and carriage also died and was never heard again.

Balfour's story didn't end there, as he ended up on the dissection table in Edinburgh and a cast was made of his head for the study of Phrenology. The cast is currently in the Collections Unit of The McManus on Barrack Street in Dundee.

BANGED **UPON** BY **AN** UNSEEN **FORCE**

EXECUTION OF DAVID BALFOUR

EXTRACT FROM BALFOUR'S LAST WORDS

"My friends, you may think that my condition is bad, and so it is; but bad as it is, I hope for mercy through the blood of my Saviour, and in his blood alone my hope rests. I hope that you will take warning from the death to which I have brought myself, and that the example that has been made of me will have a proper effect upon your minds. I regret that I have brought so much disgrace upon the town, and I am ready to die, and willing to die for it."

MARGARET BALFOUR (nee Clark) was buried in **The Howff** cemetery on **25th December 1825**

DAVID BALFOUR STABBED HIS WIFE THROUGH THE **HEART** 21ST **DECEMBER** 1825

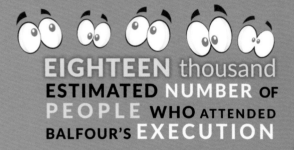

EIGHTEEN thousand **ESTIMATED NUMBER** OF **PEOPLE** WHO ATTENDED **BALFOUR'S EXECUTION**

20TH APRIL 1826 The date of **Balfour's** trial in **Perth**. It was a THURSDAY

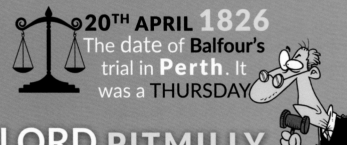

LORD PITMILLY The judge in David Balfour's trial.

Selected extracts from the "story" of Balfour's execution, The People's Journal, 29th October 1887

"...an extraordinary noise was heard, which various witnesses have described as something entirely unprecedented—not like thunder or anything with which people are familiar, but a "fearful rushing sort of sound," the origin of which is this day notwithstanding that a host of theories have been advanced on the subject. The result amongst the immense crowd which filled the High Street was as if a bombshell had suddenly burst in the midst of them. The panic began near the West end and was communicated in an instant to the whole of the dense mass, which became agitated like the waves of a tempestuous sea...Men, women, and children were seen overturned, sprawling, and screaming in all directions, while hats, caps, and bonnets separated from their owners were countless...The injuries to individuals were numerous, and some them severe, but no lives were lost. In the midst of this panic and turmoil, perhaps the most wonderful thing of all was that Balfour remained quite unmoved...although the nerves of the executioner were so unstrung that he could scarcely perform his task. It would be foolish to assert that this noise must have had supernatural origin, although that was the popular belief; but if done through human agency, the secret has been so well kept that to this day its cause has not been ascertained."

SPRING HEELS

In late 1882, from Clepington Road to Broughty Ferry, stories were multiplying of folks' encounters with a spectre by the name of Spring Heels. Said to be taller than the average Victorian man and with the ability to disappear through walls and into the shadows, Spring Heels was also said to be able to leap tall buildings, thanks to his spring-like legs.

Rumours of his appearance and his antics spread through the town until almost every detail had been embellished in some way. Spring Heels' facial features were said to be twisted and contorted. He had clawed hands and red eyes that burned as if they had been set aflame.

AS IF THEY HAD BEEN SET AFLAME

In contrast to his fiery eyes, his skin was said to be cold and clammy, like that of a corpse. The spectre's cloak was also said to be luminous, glowing from the inside as though it had been lined with phosphorous.

By the end of January 1883, after inflicting weeks of terror on men, women and children alike, the people of Dundee had had enough and set out to rid the town once and for all of any supernatural entities that dared blight their streets.

Groups of men searched into the night, but it seemed that the spectre had the good sense of mind to steer clear of the bloodthirsty band, much to their bitter disappointment.

As this search was going on, a man called William Anderson was drunkenly larking around dressed as a ghost, frightening people in the Perth Road area of the town by jumping out at them shouting and screaming.

LARKING AROUND DRESSED AS A GHOST

Thankfully for him, William wasn't caught by our mob and beaten senseless but he was picked up by the local police and thrown into jail.

The following day, a dishevelled and somewhat timid William Anderson stood before the judge and received a severe tongue-lashing before being let free without charge.

He did, however, promise never to play the part of a ghost again. Co-incidentally, the sightings of both the Blackness ghost and Spring Heels stopped...at least for a little while.

SPRING HEELS

SPRINGHEELED JACK

A supernatural Victorian urban legend originating around 1837. Springheeled Jack had all the same characteristics of the slightly renamed Spring Heels, who didn't appear in Dundee until many years later.

1867 THE YEAR SPRING HEELS MADE HIS FIRST APPEARANCE IN THE AREA

FIRST SEEN IN BROUGHTY FERRY, DECADES BEFORE THE 1882 - 1883 ENCOUNTERS

Mary Shelley, the author of Frankenstein (or The Modern Prometheus) stayed in Dundee as a guest of the Baxter family for around 18 months as a young woman between 1812 and 1814. She began writing Frankenstein in 1816 and it was first published in 1818. Mary Shelley died on 1st February 1851, aged 53.

THE OLDEST ENCOUNTER WITH A GHOST?

In the first century AD, Roman statesman Pliny the Younger reported that the spectre of an old man with a long beard and rattling chains was haunting his house in Athens.

WAS JACK BACK?

Evening Telegraph, Saturday 1st December 1900

"During the past week reports have come in from various directions which seem to indicate that someone is about playing ghostly pranks similar to the Springheel-Jack who annoyed the people of Dundee and elsewhere a number of years ago. For a time little attention was paid to the statements made by different individuals, but they have become so numerous and persistent that some credence is being paid to them. The earliest appearance of the 'ghost' in this district seems to have been on Tuesday last (27th Nov) when a farmer from the Stormont district was startled by its sudden appearance as he was driving home from market. The pony was thoroughly frightened and bolted. The cause of fright seemed a partly clad figure chiefly in white. Its next appearance was on Wed night when it suddenly appeared amongst some boys near the Public Park, Perth Road. They were at football but made a unanimous bolt...The apparition was next seen on the same night by a gentleman. On being asked where it came from, the creature indicated sulphurous regions usually associated with Old Nick which, however, did not deter the gentleman in question from applying his whip to the ghost, who disappeared as quickly as possible. It is reported to have been seen about the same road on Thursday night. A woman coming down the road was said to have been subsequently joined by the ghost. As it was very dark she was able to see little; but on making a casual remark about the weather, the apparition disappeared. A number of millworkers declared they saw the thing about Bankhead yesterday morning; and Coupar Angus, Alyth, Newtyle and Meigle seem to have had visits from it. At the last place, a girl is said to have been FRIGHTENED TO DEATH by it. The story is that the 'ghost' is a gentleman who has taken up a wage of £1000 that he will make a tour of Perthshire in disguise and escape detection. Some of the Blairgowrie lieges only wish they may have the pleasure of his company some night. They are prepared to give him a warmer reception than anything he has been accustomed to..."

Morbid Curiosities

With so many weird and wacky occurrences happening throughout Dundee's history, it's hard to fit them all into one book or a specific section. Here you'll find a selection of weird deaths, antiquated punishments, horrors of the Howff and other dark facts to tickle your pickle.

JANUaRY 1871

A girl of 3 years old had been sent upstairs by her grandmother to play with the children of their neighbour, Mrs Gibson. While the children were busy playing, Mrs Gibson was doing some washing. She set a tub of scalding-hot water on the floor and went outside to the well to fetch more water. A few moments later, she heard screams and rushed back in to find the little girl in the tub. She was so badly burned she died the following morning, 16th January 1871.

DECEmBER 1890

Martin Cox, a labourer from Dundee, was working on the whaling ship Earl of Mar and Kellie, emptying out the tanks of biscuits on the ship. While leaning into one of the large tanks to get the last of the stale biscuits from the bottom, the foul air from the tank made him dizzy and he fell inside. By the time anyone found him, he had suffocated from the noxious fumes.

FRIdAY 9TH FeBRUARY 1883

James Watt was found very dead and (mostly) lying on the rails at the south platform of the Tay Bridge Station. No one was really sure how he had ended up there, but guessed he had perhaps lain down to sleep on the rails, unaware of how dangerous his position was. A passing goods train decapitated him while he slept.

JULy 1897

Jedadiah Soutar, 59, had been blind for 3 years. Early on the morning of 7th July his wife left on an errand, leaving him some matches to light his pipe as he lay in bed. He didn't realise the match was still lit as he left it on his shirt. He set himself ablaze, dying later that afternoon from horrific injuries.

WEiRD aND UnUSUAL DEAThS

SuNDAY 8TH MaY 1898

Peter Milne, a quarryman, was found lying in the middle of the road in Kellas, the victim of a vicious beating. He was taken to Dundee Royal Infirmary where he died a few days later.

27TH OCToBER 1912

85 year old Janet Reekie was a well-known Lochee woman who always had a cheery smile for everyone. One Sunday afternoon, while eating lunch with her husband, Janet swallowed her top set of teeth. Unfortunately for her, the dental plate became lodged in her throat, cutting off her air supply. Janet was dead before she was prepared for emergency surgery at Dundee Royal Infirmary.

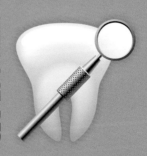

WEiRD aND UnUSUAL DEAThS

5TH DEcEMBER 1877

Francis Smart and his wife were strolling along the Esplanade beside the rail tracks when a small train engine passed, hitting Francis on the back and knocking him over the embankment. Sewer lines were being laid where he fell and he was drawn into one of them. When he re-emerged from the pipe around 30 meters down the track, he was dead.

TUESdAY 9TH mAY 1899

17 year old James Kidd was admitted to hospital after falling ill with a mysterious stomach bug on Sunday 7th May. Around 48 hours later, he was dead. The last thing he had consumed was an ice cream drink and the raspberry sauce was the supposed culprit. Tests proved nothing poisonous was in the ingredients used by the store and the shop re-opened. It was later suggested that the tools used to make the ice cream contaminated his drink, but nothing was ever proven.

DECeMBER 1909

12 year old Martha Gellatly was staying with her father on Raglan Street. She was home alone and while folding away her heavy iron bedframe, her neck got caught between the top and bottom rails as the springs quickly pulled them closed. She died of suffocation, only to be found by her father when he returned from work.

fEBRUARY 1875

ELIZABETH REW LIVED ON ANN STREET AND A FEW YEARS BEFORE THIS INCIDENT ELIZABETH HAD TRIED TO COMMIT SUICIDE BY CUTTING HER THROAT. SHE SURVIVED, BUT NEEDED A METAL PIPE IN HER THROAT TO KEEP IT OPEN AND HELP HER BREATHE. ON THIS PARTICULAR SATURDAY, SHE REMOVED THE PIPE TO CLEAN IT, SAT DOWN IN FRONT OF THE FIRE, SWIFTLY FELL ASLEEP AND BEGAN TO CHOKE. BY THE TIME HER FAMILY SUMMONED A DOCTOR, ELIZABETH WAS DEAD.

18TH JulY 1908

John Ruxton (who lived on Blackness Road in Dundee) was working on a train travelling from Aberdeen on the morning of Saturday 18th July. On route to Montrose, John climbed up a ladder to check the coal cart. As he turned to speak to his colleague, he failed to notice an overhead bridge up ahead. As he was still standing above the coal cart, his head made contact with the bridge smashing it up beyond all recognition. He died almost instantly as his colleague stood covered in bits of skull, scalp and brain matter!

REPENTANCE

For most crimes dealt with by the church, you'd have to publicly repent and apologise for your sins to the entire congregation, who were your neighbours, friends and family.

As well as apologising you'd also have to spend a few hours publicly chained up. Stocks and pillories were most often used for men, whereas women would normally end up chained to a stool by the arms or legs. Sometimes you were made to remain standing by the Tron (town weighing scales) by having your ear nailed to it!

More serious offences warranted more humiliation and sometimes offenders had to wear nothing but sackcloth while admitting their guilt, such as a cheating tax collector who had to appear before the provost in a sack, barefoot and bare-headed. In 1551, a woman was made to walk through the centre of Dundee on her knees with a rosary around her heels.

PUNISHMENTS

BRANKS / SCOLD'S BRIDLE

Branks were used mainly on women in the 16th and 17th centuries for crimes such as slander, gossiping or 'troublesome' speech, but were sometimes used on men. You could also end up in the branks in Dundee if you were caught disposing of 'filth' in the streets or any public space.

It was a form of torture and public humiliation as you would be made to sit on the 'cuck-stule', the stool fixed near the Tolbooth, during the busiest times of day whilst wearing it for all to see.

MADE OF IRON, BRANKS WERE LIKE A CAGE ENCLOSING THE HEAD. A BRIDLE-BIT OR IRON PLATE WOULD GO INTO THE MOUTH, PRESSING DOWN ON THE TONGUE TO PREVENT SPEAKING BUT ALSO TO CAUSE EXCESSIVE SALIVATION AND ORAL FATIGUE, FURTHER EMBARRASSING THE OFFENDER

1567 BRANKS FIRST USED IN SCOTLAND AS A FORM OF PUNISHMENT

BANISHMENT

This was the harshest punishment that could be handed out, besides execution. The unfortunate people banished from their homes were easy prey for thieves and bandits. Other towns were wary of strangers and would often shun banished people and bar them entry.

If anyone banished from Dundee tried to return before their time was up, or return at all if they were banished for life, they would be whipped and branded with the town's branding iron on the cheek before being cast out again. Any further attempt to return would see you executed.

GRAHAM SUTHEL was banished from Dundee for 'irregular practices' in **April 1780,** ELIZABETH OGILVIE was banished for receiving stolen goods in **November 1784** and JOHN ORCHARD, a sailor caught breaking into a ship's cabin and stealing clothes in **November 1784** was also banished from the town.

PUNISHMENTS

WHIPPING

Lashes were dealt out by the town hangman to men and women and how hard he might lash you depended on the public mood. Often two or three strapped leather whips or belts would be used.

No matter how harsh the physical punishment, it was still not seen to be as bad a sentence as banishment. In 1553, James Richardson was accused of theft in Dundee. As it couldn't be proven, he couldn't be banished from the town, but instead received the 'lesser' punishment of 12 strokes with a double belt.

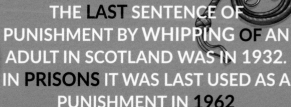

THE **LAST** SENTENCE OF PUNISHMENT BY WHIPPING OF AN ADULT IN SCOTLAND WAS IN 1932. IN **PRISONS** IT WAS LAST USED AS A PUNISHMENT IN **1962**

BONNIE SUSIE CLELAND

- SONG, FIRST PUBLISHED BY WILLIAM MOTHERWELL IN HIS 'MINSTRELSY ANCIENT AND MODERN' (1827)

Based on an older song called 'Lady Maisery' there is a bit of a legend behind this heartbreaking song. There is a local traditional tale that many women were killed for consorting with English soldiers who were stationed in the town for 9 years after the storming of Dundee by General Monck in 1651. Burning or hanging was also the prescribed penalty in medieval Scottish law for sexual indulgence by an unmarried woman unless her family protected the offender or found a father for her child. The cruelty of the family in the ballad in burning their own daughter is unimaginable. Whether real or not, it's hard to read the lyrics and not feel awful for poor Susie Cleland.

There lived a lady in Scotland
Hey my love, ho my joy
There lived a lady in Scotland
So dearly she loved me
There lived a lady in Scotland
She fell in love with an Englishman
Bonnie Susie Cleland, she's to be burned in Dundee

The father to his daughter came
Will you forsake this Englishman?
If you will not this Englishman forsake
Then I will burn you at the stake

Where may I find a pretty little boy
To carry tokens to my joy
Bring to him this right hand glove
Tell him to find another love

Bring to him this wee pen knife
Tell him to find another wife
Bring to him this gay gold ring
Tell him I'm going to my burning

The father he put up the stake
The brothers the fire did make
Bonnie Susie Cleland, she was burned at Dundee

DRAWING BY STELLAR LEUNA

CRIMES OF THE 1500's

It was illegal to be caught on the streets after 10pm. No one was allowed to walk around at night without a lantern and without being on official business. A fine was the punishment for the first offence, with banishment for the second.

Drinking after 9pm and selling anyone alcohol after 9pm was strictly forbidden, although selling it was worse. Although the drunk would get a fine for the first offence, the alcohol seller would be immediately banished!

Alexander Clarke and Elizabeth Stevenson were both banished from the town in 1550 for various misdemeanours which included theft but also being out at night continuously.

9pm to 10pm was definitely quiet time. If you were found outside your house dancing or playing music, your instruments would be broken to bits and you would be thrown in jail until you paid a 20 shilling fine.

Drunkenness in general was also a crime, with a small fine for the first and second offence. The third would be a £10 fine (over £5,000 in 2020) and if they continued, they would be banished for a year and a day and only allowed back inside the town if they showed repentance.

Blasphemy and swearing (or 'evil speech') were also big crimes in the 1500's. If you were caught, you could pay a fine, 2 shillings for the first offence and 20 for the second. If you couldn't pay, you had to spend 2 hours for your first offence, or 6 hours for your second, in the 'branks' or scold's bridle. Third offence was banishment, whether you were poor or rich.

Anyone caught for prostitution or running a brothel had 24 hours to leave town, otherwise they would be brought before the Mercat Cross and banished publicly.

IN THE **12TH CENTURY**, A WOMAN CALLED **DEVORGILLA**, MOTHER OF FUTURE-KING **JOHN BALLIOL**, FOUNDED A MONASTERY FOR THE **GREY** OR **FRANCISCAN** FRIARS ON THE SITE OF WHAT IS NOW **THE HOWFF**

In the middle of the Protestant Reformation in the 1540's, many townsfolk in Dundee had been whipped up into a frenzy and took it upon themselves to storm the monasteries, run the monks out of town and loot their buildings.

1564

The area was left to **ruin** and rubble for just over two decades until it was granted as a place of burial in **1564** by Mary Queen of Scots.

HORRORS OF THE HOWFF

MEETING PLACE

The word howff (or houff) means meeting place, or comfortable meeting place and usually referred to alehouses. Getting drunk at every meeting wasn't working well for the 9 trades of Dundee, so they paid the council to use the burial ground as their meeting place, referred to it as 'the Howff' in 1576 and the name stuck.

£5 PER YEAR

THE FEE PAID BY THE NINE TRADES TO THE COUNCIL FOR THE HONOUR OF HANGING OUT IN A CEMETERY. THAT'S WELL OVER £2,000 IN 2020!

In the early days, the Howff was a lush, open space. People would also use the area to dry their washing, sometimes using the rougher gravestones to scrub their clothes as well as grazing their livestock within the burial grounds! In the 1700's, a law had to be put in place to issue fines to anyone allowing their horses or other animals in the Howff at all.

GETTING THE BOAK MEANS TO FEEL SICK, WHICH IS HOW A LOT OF PEOPLE FELT ABOUT THE HOWFF

Before the Howff closed to burials in 1860 a hearing was held about the problems being reported about the Howff and the residents around it had plenty to say. The overpowering smell, they said, was of decaying animals, not sewerage as others had tried to claim. They complained that the stench seemed to come up from the ground underneath the floors and cellars of their buildings, making them feel nauseated and in some cases vomit because it was so pungent. When graves were being dug on the east side during wet winters when waterlogging was particularly bad, a thick, black, tar-like substance would pour from the coffins next to the grave being dug. The gravediggers needed extra money and a dram of whisky to keep going and they were repeatedly sick.

It was said that no part of the Howff could be dug up without coming across either thick creamy-looking matter (possibly grave wax) or partly decayed body parts.

HORRORS OF THE HOWFF

IT IS **ESTIMATED** THAT THERE COULD BE ANYWHERE FROM **80,000** TO **100,000** BODIES BURIED IN THE **HOWFF** CEMETERY. THERE ARE **CURRENTLY** AROUND 1750 VISIBLE GRAVESTONES

There have been many unofficial burials in the Howff cemetery. James Kettle, superintendent of the burying ground said in 1858 that in the previous 11 years, he had seen hundreds of people buried there who had no rights to the plots.

When the Howff was first used as a burying ground it wasn't secure and its ruinous walls were also the town boundary walls. You could easily sneak into or out of town over the Howff walls, so it quickly became a crime, punishable with an 8 shilling fine. It didn't stop people however and the council moved the town gate back to in-line with the Howff south wall and rebuilt it in 1601.

"SINCE THE **HOWFF** WAS CLOSED AS A **PLACE** FOR **BURIALS**, IT HAS **BECOME** A SINK OF IMPURITY, FOR **MEN** AND **WOMEN** MAKE IT A PLACE OF **RENDEZVOUS**, WHERE SCENES ARE EXHIBITED IN FORMS THAT I **WILL** NOT ATTEMPT TO **DESCRIBE**..."

Part of a letter written to the Dundee, Perth and Cupar Advertiser printed Tuesday 11th June 1861 by a neighbour of the Howff.

At night, locals would gather in the Howff to drink alcohol and gamble. Gambling was a huge problem, with dozens of men gathered there most nights to bet on anything from bare-knuckle fighting to more brutal 'games' involving tying animals such as chickens and roosters to stakes and then taking turns in beating them to death.

HORRORS OF THE HOWFF

A SMASHING TIME

WE MADE THE MOST OF SPACE IN THE HOWFF USING A VARIETY OF METHODS INCLUDING LAYING GRAVES CLOSER TOGETHER, NOT BURYING THEM TOO DEEP AND SMASHING UP THE COFFINS TO MAKE ROOM FOR MORE DEAD PEOPLE!

Saturday 4th May 1919 was a particularly busy day. With someone selling bottles of methylated spirits in the Howff, the local drunks were more than keen to get their hands on it. By lunchtime, 4 people had been arrested. John Murray, 55, had to be carted away in a wheelbarrow to get his stomach pumped!

EXTRACTS FROM AN ARTICLE IN THE DUNDEE, PERTH AND CUPAR ADVERTISER, 20TH MARCH 1860:

"Horrors of the Howff... we have just seen a man digging up large pieces of a comparatively new coffin... breaking up into bits that look like fresh cut firewood... an old man publicly employed in disinterring one dead person to make room in the same grave for a new claimant... Here the dead man is grudged his few feet of earth..."

BY 1934, THE PARKS COMMITTEE MADE THE DECISION TO CLOSE THE HOWFF DURING RACING HOURS